Clearly Social Studies

Grade 4

Author: Marsha Elyn Wright
Editors: Stephanie Garcia, Bob Newman, Todd Sharp
Cover Designer: Anthony D. Paular
Interior Designer: Anthony D. Paular
Interior Artist: Marilee Harrald-Pilz

Frank Schaffer Publications®

Judy/Instructo is an imprint of Frank Schaffer Publications.

Send all inquiries to:
Frank Schaffer Publications
8720 Orion Place
Columbus OH, 43240-2111

ISBN: 0-7682-0632-4

4 5 6 7 8 9 10 MAZ 10 09 08 07 06

TABLE OF CONTENTS

Introduction 3

U.S. Geography

Teacher Ideas and Activities............................4–5

"Travelin' Tourists" Bulletin Board.......................5

Five Regions of the United States
(Map skills) 6

Our Country's Natural Riches
(Map reading, Charts) 7

Protecting Our Resources (Comprehension,
Making a chart) 8

The West (Using a physical map).....................9

The Southwest
(Measuring with a map scale) 10

The Midwest
(Recognizing time zones).......................11

The Southeast
(Using latitude and longitude) 12

The Northeast (Using a compass rose) 13

The Beginning of America

Teacher Ideas and Activities........................14–15

"Let's Go Exploring" Bulletin Board 15

Cultural Areas of North American Indians
(Comprehension, Identification)................16

Sailing to the Americas in 1492
(Cause and effect) 17

Spanish Explorers and Conquistadors
(Using map symbols, Comprehension) 18

Around the World
(Using a historical map)........................19

Life on a Spanish Mission
(Using a map grid)...............................20

Fighting for North America
(Using historical maps) 21

Breaking Away From British Rule
(Reading a time line) 22

The American Revolution
(Comprehension, Application)...................23

Declaration of Independence
(Making inferences, Supporting opinions)...........24

The Constitution of the United States
(Reading for details)............................25

Rights, Rights, Rights (Fact and opinion).............26

The First U.S. President (Stating opinions,
Supporting answers)...............................27

A Time of Growth

Teacher Ideas and Activities........................28–29

"Banners of Bold Americans" Bulletin Board............29

Jefferson Expands the U.S.A. (Comprehension,
Making a time line)...............................30

Lewis and Clark Go Exploring (Reading primary
sources, Proofreading, Creative thinking).............31

Going on an Expedition (Organizing information,
Writing a paragraph, Speaking)...................32

The Pathfinder (Comprehension) 33

Two Presidents Named James (Compare and
contrast, Application).............................34

Jackson Brings Growth and Tears (Context clues,
Definitions)......................................35

A Changing Way of Life

Teacher Ideas and Activities 36–37

"Zip! Pop! Inventions" Bulletin Board..................37

The Industrial Revolution
(Comprehension, Critical thinking)................38

Moving Right Along . . . (Cause and effect) 39

Pioneers Go Far West (Reading a map)................40

The Rush for Gold! (Making a web map,
Creative writing)................................41

The War Between the States (Comprehension,
Critical thinking)................................42

Rebuilding a Country
(Vocabulary, Critical thinking).....................43

Studying Any State

Teacher Ideas and Activities........................44–45

"Our GREAT State News" Bulletin Board..............45

State Reference Chart (Reading a chart) 46

United States Map (Reading a map).................47

State Poster Planning Guide (Research,
Recording information)...........................48

State Map Grid (Making a map grid,
Research) 49

State Flag (Comprehension, Research)...............50

A Road Map (Using a road map).....................51

State Group Work (Group work)....................52

Create a State (Planning, Critical thinking,
Mapmaking) 53

Answers..54

Transparencies

T1: United States Regions..............................57

T2: United States Physical Map........................58

T3: Graphic Organizers.................................59

T4: Web Mapping.......................................60

T5: The United States..................................61

T6: United States Political Map........................62

T7: Latitude and Longitude 63

T8: World Physical Map................................64

INTRODUCTION

Clearly Social Studies is designed to help your students develop an understanding of basic social studies concepts taught in fourth grade: the geography of the United States; geographic regions; linking major events in American history with the contemporary world; understanding the growth of the United States from Native Americans to early explorers and pioneers; and an in-depth study of the students' home state. Focus areas of study complement the NCSS (National Council for the Social Studies) *Curriculum Standards for Social Studies*.

Clearly Social Studies encourages the students to broaden their sense of self. The students will begin to connect with the world around them and the people and events that have made a difference in history. Questions are provided, both in the activities and on the reproducibles, that can be used as springboards for rich classroom discussions. The activities in **Clearly Social Studies** help the students apply their skills and knowledge in a variety of formats and presentations. These activities can be used all year to captivate students and enrich your social studies instruction!

Clearly Social Studies content areas of study are separated into different strands featuring art and hands-on, concept-building activities as well as several reproducibles. As an added bonus, **Clearly Social Studies** features a collection of *full-color transparencies* for use throughout the book. Use the transparencies as is, or duplicate and distribute them to the students. Activities designed for use with specific transparencies are marked accordingly. Some activities use two transparencies—one for the overhead and one as an overlay to use in tandem with the first transparency. With these transparencies, you are all set for a successful lesson that requires little preparation time for you!

Clearly Social Studies contains bulletin board display ideas and activities to enhance each unit of study. These are featured and described at the beginning of each unit. Each display is designed to be created by both you and your students for a cooperative effort.

Clearly Social Studies can begin with the motivational bulletin board display described below!

Student-made collage of items that help identify a specific state

Suitcase pattern 17" x 22"

Pack Up for America!

Post a United States map on a wall or bulletin board. Make a simple suitcase pattern on a sheet of 17" x 22" paper and copy the pattern so that each student has one. Pin the "empty" suitcases near the map. Let each student choose a state to "visit" and discover what is special about that state. Have each child create a montage on a suitcase about his or her state during your study of the United States. When a student learns something about his or her state, the student can draw a picture, cut out a magazine photo, or attach a symbolic item (such as a peanut for Georgia) on his or her suitcase. By the end of your study, the suitcases should be packed with exciting information about each state chosen! You may want to pin a length of string from the suitcase to the corresponding state on the map.

U.S. GEOGRAPHY

As the students study the different regions and geography of the United States, they will better understand the geography and culture of their home state.

Regions of the United States in Song

Transparency 1

Begin your study of the United States by teaching your students this simple song about U.S. regions. Display Transparency 1, *United States Regions*. After your students sing the song, see if they can identify on the transparency map the specific mountain ranges, great rivers, and coastal low lands that the song describes for the various regions.

"Sing a Song of Regions"
(Sung to the tune of "Sing a Song of Sixpence")

Sing a song of regions,
Of five regions in all,
West and Southwest regions,
With mountains tall,
Midwest with vast plains,
Southeast with rivers great,
Northeast with coastal lowlands make up the 50 states!

Ask the students general questions about the five U.S. regions to help the students learn to differentiate them. Ask questions such as the following: *Which regions have the greatest number of states? Which region has the fewest number of states? Which regions have coastal areas? Which region shares its borders with four other regions?* Then challenge the boys to ask the girls creative questions about the map. Have the students switch roles so that the girls do the asking next.

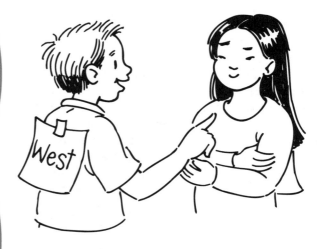

Which Region Am I?

Play this geography game to help the students better identify the different regions. Write the names of the five regions on separate sheets of paper and display these labels on the walls around the classroom. Also write each region name on separate index cards. Make enough cards for the entire class. Tape a card to the back of each student. Try to have an equal number of students for each region. Set a time limit for the students to walk around and ask their classmates yes-or-no questions to help identify which regions are taped to their backs. When a student guesses correctly, he or she stands by the corresponding regional label in the classroom. When the time is up, see how many students were able to identify their regions!

Calling All Tourists!

Place the students in five different groups and assign each group a region of the United States. Tell the students that it is up to them to learn some interesting facts about their regions. They can use atlases, encyclopedias, magazines, and library books. Challenge each group to create a visitor's guide for its region. Let the students have plenty of time for researching, writing, and illustrating their guides. Have each group pretend to be tour guides and try to convince the rest of the class to visit their region. See which group makes the best pitch!

Weather Watch

Share that the United States has a varied climate. Tell the students that they will be in charge of reporting the weather for the entire country each week. Place the students in five groups of reporters. Assign each group a specific week in which to report the weather. Tell the reporters to locate the weather report in a newspaper, on the Internet, and/or on television and take notes. Have the reporters get together the next day to make maps and charts as well as decide how to arrange the room into a TV station format. As students listen to the daily classroom weather reports, have them keep track of the weather in specific regions. After several weeks, have them predict the weather in their regions based on the trends they observe.

America the Amazing

After the students learn about the various regions of the United States, write a class song about what makes America special. Use the tune to "America the Beautiful." Write the class song on chart paper, and have the students draw a large mural illustrating the new words to their song. Perform the song for another class. Make sure to display the mural while singing the song.

Wild About Recycling

Talk with the students about how important it is for everyone to work together to conserve America's natural resources—water, air, forests, minerals. Remind the students that one way to conserve resources is to recycle. Declare one of the school months Recycling Awareness Month. Have your class design posters about conservation and recycling and post them around the school.

Travelin' Tourists

Child's self-portrait as a tourist

tagboard child pattern

Let the students' imagination go wild as they create portraits of themselves as tourists. Make a large (two-foot-tall) child pattern out of tagboard. Let each student trace the pattern onto butcher paper and cut it out. Ask the parents to donate fabric scraps, buttons, and other decorative items. Let each student decorate a child pattern to look like himself or herself as a tourist. Encourage the students to add hair, faces, clothes, hats, shoes, cameras, suitcases, sunglasses, and whatever else might be useful to take on a vacation. After each student shares his or her tourist creation, let the student tell where he or she would like to travel in the United States and why.

Name **Morgan** 4-29-16

Five Regions of the United States

Follow the directions to color this map of the United States to show its five regions:

1. Color states in the West red.
2. Color states in the Midwest brown.
3. Color states in the Northeast green.
4. Color states in the Southwest yellow.
5. Color states in the Southeast orange.
6. Color stripes on your state.

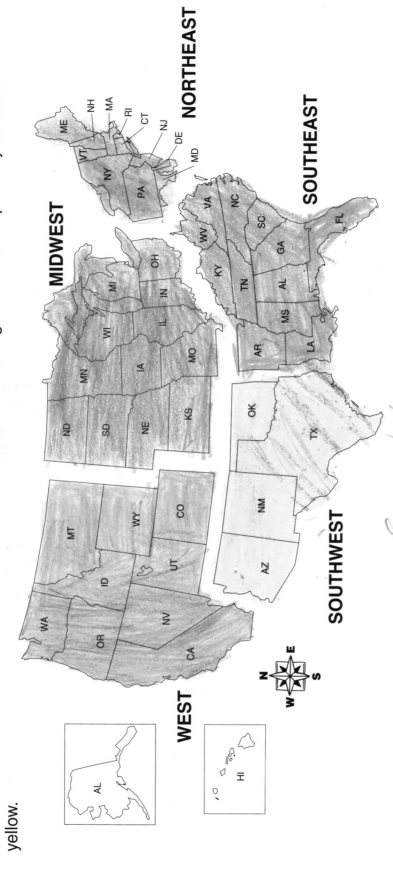

7. Which region has the fewest states? _Southwest_
8. In what state do you live? _TX_
9. In which region is your state? _Southwest_
10. List three other states in your region: _Ok, AZ, NM_

J332004 Clearly Social Studies

Our Country's Natural Riches

Many materials in nature help us live better lives. These materials are called **natural resources**. Some natural resources, such as coal and oil, cannot be replaced. Other resources, such as trees, can be replaced. All natural resources need to be protected. Use the map to find the 16 missing natural resources. Write them on the chart.

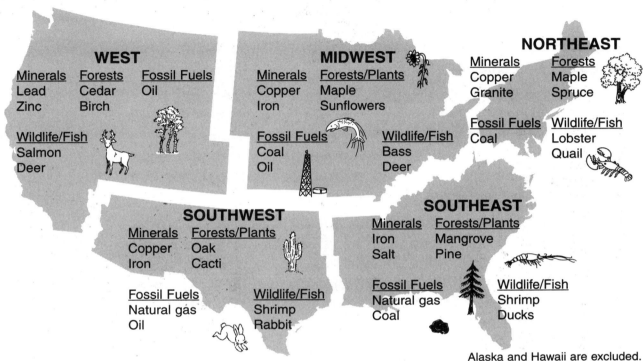

WEST

Minerals	Forests	Fossil Fuels
Lead	Cedar	Oil
Zinc	Birch	

Wildlife/Fish
Salmon
Deer

MIDWEST

Minerals	Forests/Plants
Copper	Maple
Iron	Sunflowers

Fossil Fuels	Wildlife/Fish
Coal	Bass
Oil	Deer

NORTHEAST

Minerals	Forests
Copper	Maple
Granite	Spruce

Fossil Fuels	Wildlife/Fish
Coal	Lobster
	Quail

SOUTHWEST

Minerals	Forests/Plants
Copper	Oak
Iron	Cacti

Fossil Fuels	Wildlife/Fish
Natural gas	Shrimp
Oil	Rabbit

SOUTHEAST

Minerals	Forests/Plants
Iron	Mangrove
Salt	Pine

Fossil Fuels	Wildlife/Fish
Natural gas	Shrimp
Coal	Ducks

Alaska and Hawaii are excluded.

Natural Resources of the United States Regions				
REGION	**FOSSIL FUELS**	**FORESTS/PLANTS**	**MINERALS**	**WILDLIFE/FISH**
WEST	Oil	birch Cedar	Lead zinc	Deer salmon
MIDWEST	Oil Coal	Maple Sunflowers	Copper Iron	Deer Bass
SOUTHWEST	Natural gas Oil	Cacti Oak	Iron Copper	Rabbit shrimp
NORTHEAST	Coal	Maple Spruce	granite Copper	Quail lobsters
SOUTHEAST	Natural gas coal	Pine Mangrove	Iron salt	Ducks Shrimp

Morgan 2-11-17

Protecting Our Resources

Read the information. Complete the chart using the **boldfaced** words and phrases.

The United States has many natural resources. Fossil fuels are widely used resources. They come from plant and animal fossils and include coal, oil, and natural gas. They **heat our homes** and **run our vehicles and machines**. But we are **using them up fast**. They cannot be renewed! We need to **set limits** on the number of fossil fuels taken from the earth. We need to **conserve** our fuels, being careful to turn down our heat and turn off lights.

Forests are a valuable resource. Trees **soak up sunlight** so that the earth doesn't get too hot. They **produce oxygen**. Trees are **made into paper goods**. But **insects and diseases** threaten our forests. Chemicals we use mix with the air and form **acid rain**, which poisons our trees. We need to **limit the chemicals we use**. We need to cut down fewer trees by **recycling paper**.

Another useful resource is soil. It's needed for **growing crops, plants, and trees**. But we deplete the soil by **planting too many crops**. **Acid rain** poisons the soil. We need to **use less chemicals** and **control the amount of crops** we grow. We need to **put nutrients back into the soil** to restore it. Protecting our natural resources is an important job for all of us.

Natural Resources	Usefulness/ Value	Things That Threaten	How to Protect/ Conserve
Fossil Fuels	Heat our homes run our vehicles and Machines	We're using them up Fast.	Set limits Conserve
Forests	Soak up sunlight Produce oxygen make into paper goods	insects and diseases acid rain	limit the chemicals we use recycling paper
Soil	crops plants and trees	Planting too many crops, acid rain	use less chemicals to control the amount of crops

J332004 Clearly Social Studies

Name Morgan 2-11-17

The West

Geography is the study of our planet and how we live on it and use it. To help us study the geography of the United States, people have divided the country into five regions. One of the regions is the West. Below is a physical map of the Western region. It shows rivers, mountains, lakes and other landforms. Use the map to answer the questions in complete sentences.

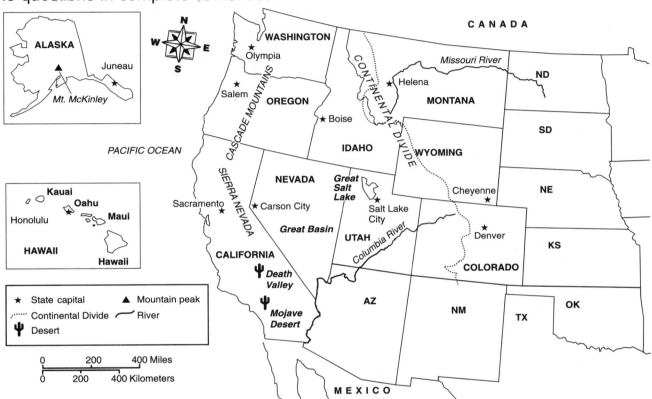

1. An imaginary line through the Rocky Mountains divides the country in half. Rivers west of the line flow toward the Pacific Ocean. Rivers to the east drain into either the Atlantic Ocean or the Gulf of Mexico. What is the name of this line? _Its called a continental Divide_

2. Which state capital is near a large lake? _The answer is The salt Lak city_

3. The tallest mountain in the United States is in Alaska. What is its name? _Its name is mt McKinley_

4. Which river flows near the capital of Montana? _The missouri river_

5. What are two deserts in the Great Basin? _Theres Mojave desert and Death valley_

The Southwest

All maps show an area that is larger than the map itself. Each map has a scale. The scale shows the relationship between the real distances and the places on the map. Follow these directions to make a scale strip:

1. Place the edge of a strip of paper under the scale lines on the map below.
2. Use your pencil to mark the distances in miles on your strip.
3. Slide your strip. Keep marking miles until your strip can measure the whole map.
4. Place the opposite edge under the scales of lines and mark kilometers.

Use your scale strip to answer these questions on the back of this paper.

1. On a trip from the capital of Arizona to the capital of New Mexico, about how many miles would you have to travel?

2. About how many kilometers is Austin, Texas, from where the Rio Grande and Pecos rivers meet?

3. If you started in Santa Fe and traveled west about 300 kilometers, would you reach the Grand Canyon or the Painted Desert?

4. If you left Oklahoma City and drove south toward Austin, Texas, would you have reached Austin if you ran out of gas 300 miles south of Oklahoma City?

5. What is a landform you could explore about 200 kilometers from Phoenix?

6. Plan a car trip from Phoenix to Oklahoma City. About how many miles would you travel between the two cities?

J332004 Clearly Social Studies

The Midwest

The Midwest is known for its rich farmlands. It's often called the "Corn Belt" because of all the corn grown there. The Midwest also has three different time zones. Use this time zone map to answer the questions in complete sentences.

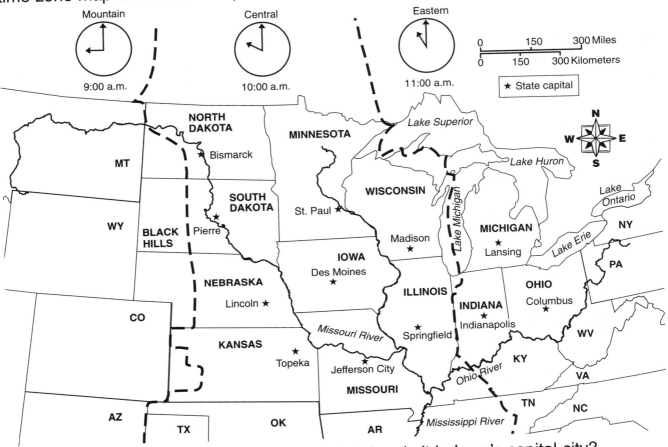

1. If it's 10:00 a.m. in Topeka, Kansas, what time is it in Iowa's capital city?

2. If it's 3:00 p.m. in Lincoln, Nebraska, what time is it in Indianapolis, Indiana?

3. When school in Columbus, Ohio, begins at 8:00 a.m., what time is it for schoolchildren living near the Black Hills in South Dakota? _____

4. Can you find three states with two time zones? Write their names. _____

5. If you lived in Lansing, Michigan, and a friend in St. Paul, Minnesota, asked you to call at 7:00 p.m. her time, what time would you phone her from your house?

J332004 Clearly Social Studies

The Southeast

The Southeast is known for its big river—the Mississippi. This river creates rich farmlands. Below is a map that shows latitude and longitude lines. These lines help us locate places on a map. **Latitude** lines run east and west. The starting line is the **equator** at 0° latitude, halfway between the north and south poles. **Longitude** lines run north and south. The starting line is the **prime meridian** at 0° longitude. Use the map to answer the questions.

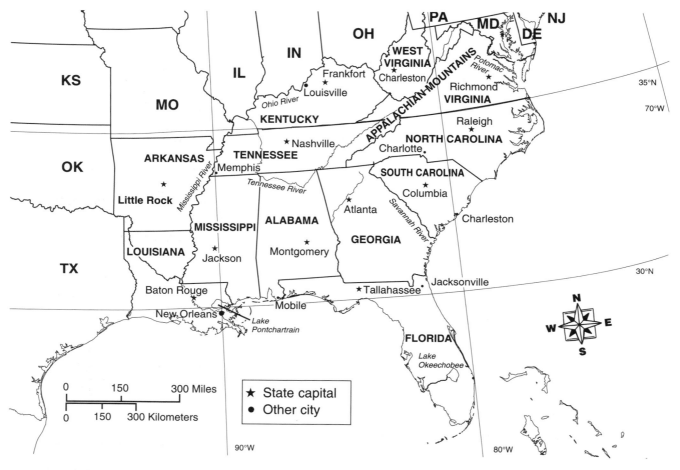

1. Which city is at 30°N and 90°W? _____

2. Which river runs near the 90°W longitude line? _____

3. Kentucky is between which longitude lines? _____

4. Which lake is south of the 30°N latitude line? _____

5. Which state capital is nearest the same line of longitude as New Orleans?

   _____

6. Can you think of your own map question? Write it. Have a classmate answer it.

The Northeast

The Northeast is the smallest region, but it has a varied landscape of coastal plains, hills, and mountains. Use the compass rose on the map to answer the questions. A **compass rose** shows **cardinal directions**—**n**orth, **s**outh, **e**ast, and **w**est. Often it also shows **intermediate directions**, those that are in between the cardinal directions—northwest, southwest, northeast, and southeast.

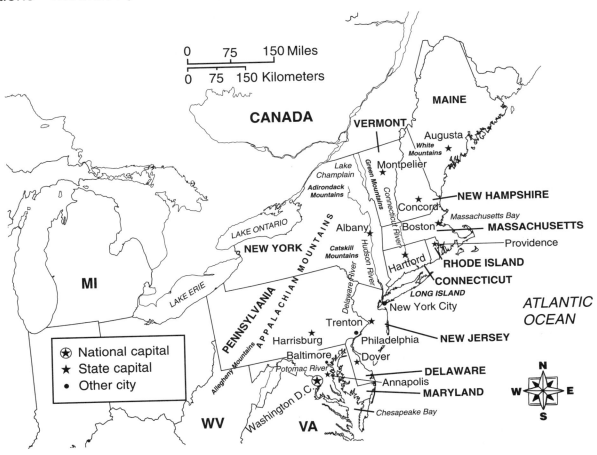

1. In what direction is Long Island from Connecticut? _____

2. In what direction are the Green Mountains from New Hampshire? _____

3. Which state capital is northeast of Philadelphia? _____

4. Which states are along New York's eastern border? _____

   _____

5. Which state capital is southeast of Harrisburg? _____

6. Which capital is southwest of Baltimore? _____

7. Can you think of your own map question? Write it. Have a classmate answer it.

   _____

J332004 Clearly Social Studies

THE BEGINNING OF AMERICA

Help the students better understand how America was shaped by Native Americans, early explorers, and New England colonists.

Native Americans Long Ago and Now

Begin your study of the United States by sharing some books about Native Americans:

- *People of the Breaking Day* by Marcia Sewall (Atheneum, 1990)

- *Powwow* by George Ancona (Harcourt Brace Jovanovich, 1993)

- *Pueblo Storyteller* by Diane Hoyt-Goldsmith (Holiday House, 1991)

- *The Goat in the Rug* by Charles L. Blood and Martin Link (Macmillan, 1984)

- *Raven* by Gerald McDermott (Harcourt Brace Jovanovich, 1993)

Guide your students in understanding that long ago people lived in small groups all across North America. Explain that where they lived determined the food they ate, the kind of homes they built, and the clothing they wore. Reproduce page 16 and do the activity about the different Native American cultural areas of North America.

Geography Plays a Big Role

Transparency 2

Display Transparency 2, *United States Physical Map*. Discuss the landforms shown on the map. Place the students into six groups. Assign each group a different Native American cultural area—Far North, Eastern Woodlands, Plains, Far West, Southwest, and Northwest. (The map and activity on page 16 is a good resource.) Talk about how the Native Americans in each area adapted to their environments. Explain that it is the job of each group to make a poster that describes the geography and environment of its cultural area. Let the students use the transparency map and other physical maps to find their information.

Emphasize the role geography played in Native Americans' lives. As each group shares its poster, invite the class to ask questions of the group: *What kinds of food did the Native Americans living in your area eat? What were their homes made of?*

Northwest Coast Carvings

Share this information with your students: *For hundreds of years, Native Americans of the Northwest Coast carved totem poles. These totem poles told the history of a tribe or family. Totems are animals or objects that are important to a tribe. In the past, Native Americans carved totem poles at the front of their wooden houses so that the poles faced the ocean and visitors arriving by water could see them.* If possible, share some pictures of totem poles. Then have each student make a model of a totem pole by following these directions.

Materials:
- empty oatmeal container
- tempera paints and brush
- sturdy construction paper scraps
- newspaper
- scissors
- pencil, black marker
- masking tape or glue

Directions:
1. Paint the oatmeal container a color. Let it dry.
2. List the animals that you will draw and use on your totem pole. (Choose from these: eagle, owl, bear, whale, fish, salmon, beaver, wolf, frog, and raven.)
3. Draw each of the animals on separate scraps to make your totems. Using black marker, trace over your outline of each animal.
4. Cut out each animal. Arrange the animals (one on top of the other) on one side of the oatmeal container. If you need to, make more totems. Once you have an arrangement, glue the totems in place and color them.

Classroom Primers

Share stories such as the following:

- *Colonial Life* by Bobbie Kalman (Crabtree, 1992)
- *If You Lived in Colonial Times* by Ann McGovern (Scholastic, 1992)
- *The Sign of the Beaver* by Elizabeth George Speare (Houghton Mifflin, 1983)

Tell your students that in colonial days after young children learned to read and write, only the boys continued going to school; the girls stayed home. The only schoolbook for the boys was the *New England Primer*. It contained prayers as well as rhymes for each letter of the alphabet: *A Dog will bite a thief at night.* Invite the students to write their own *Primer.* Assign small groups of students sets of alphabet letters. Have every group write a poem on a separate sheet of paper for each of its letters and illustrate the poem. Then compile the pages into a class book. Let the students take turns reading the book to a primary class in your school.

Organizing Information

Display Transparency 3, which features two graphic organizers—*Horizontal Chart* and *Cause and Effect Chart*. As the children study the different early explorers of North America, have them compile and compare information about the people and events on these different graphic organizers. For example, write a different explorer's name in each of the top boxes on the Horizontal Chart. Play a review game. Place your students in three groups and assign each group a different explorer. Challenge the groups to list on paper facts they can recall about their explorers. Give them 5 to 10 minutes. When time is up, have a representative from each group list three facts on the transparency.

List two events that happened in early America (Columbus's landing and settlers building Jamestown) under *Causes* on the Causes and Effects organizer. Ask questions such as the following: *What were the effects of Columbus's landing in the New World—to the Native Americans, to future colonists, to Columbus?* For each event, see how many effects the students can think of.

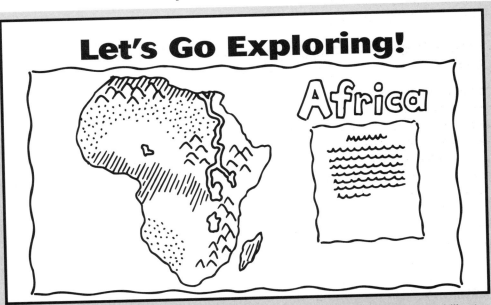

Group model map of a place to explore

Group report

Place the students in small groups. Have each group choose a place on earth where they would like to explore now. Direct each group to create a large map on butcher paper that shows the place of exploration. Have the groups color their maps to show lakes, mountains, forests, deserts, and other landforms. Have each group write a paragraph that describes why it would want to explore this area. After each group shares its paragraph and map, display them together.

Name _Morgan_____

Cultural Areas of North American Indians

Different tribes of Indians living in a certain area formed a similar culture, or way of life. Read the chart. Identify each of the six cultural areas on the map. Write its name in the correct box. Choose a different color for each cultural area. Color the map.

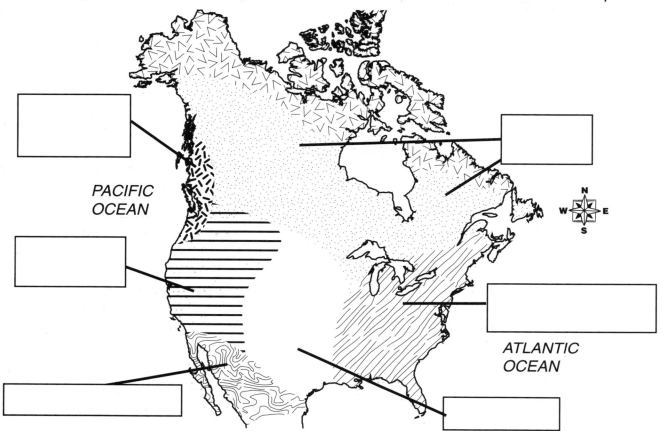

Cultural Area	Description
FAR NORTH	lakes and rivers; long, cold, snowy winters; tundra; forests; invented toboggans and snowshoes; in summer used canoes
NORTHWEST COAST	rivers; forests; coastal lands; mild climate; hunted whales for food and oil; built cedar houses; carved totem poles
EASTERN WOODLANDS	forests; mountains; lakes; coastal land; cold winters in the north; skilled hunters, fishermen, and farmers
SOUTHWEST	deserts; mesas; canyons; very dry climate; skilled craftsmen; many had to move from place to place to find food
FAR WEST	mountains and plateaus; desert area; lots of plants; rivers; gathered food such as acorns, seeds, plants; hunted; fished
PLAINS	grasslands; prairies; few trees; buffalo hunters; followed where herds moved; lived in portable homes or "tepees"

J332004 Clearly Social Studies

Sailing to the Americas in 1492

Read the stories below. Under *Causes* on the chart, write a phrase describing an event from each story. Think about the effects of each event. Write them on the chart.

We are Taino (TI noh). We are island people. We catch fish. We carve out trees to make canoes. We weave plants into string to make a bed called a hamaca (hammock).

One day, strange men sailed to our islands. One of us cut his hand on a stranger's sharp spear! We gave the strangers our wooden spears, balls of thread, and parrots. They gave us glass beads and tiny bells. We welcomed the strangers. But they forced several of us to sail back with them on their boat!

Now more strangers come. They bring strange things. They build homes on our land and make us work for them. Our people die from their diseases. Soon, I fear, we will be no more.

I am Christopher Columbus. The king and queen of Spain paid me to find a new way to Asia to bring its gold and riches back to Spain!

"*¡Tierra! ¡Tierra!*" shouts a sailor. I see land. It must be an island near Asia. I will call it *San Salvador*, or Holy Savior, and claim it for Spain. We are greeted by friendly natives. I call them *Indios* since they live here in the Indies. They are poor. They trade us many things for our bells and beads. They should make fine servants because they learn quickly. I will take some of them back to Spain. I will take back new things I see here—turkeys, potatoes, corn, and tobacco. Then I will return with more ships and bring horses, cattle, sheep, and seeds for growing sugar cane, onions, and wheat. I will build colonies!

CAUSES	EFFECTS
	_____ _____
	_____ _____

Name ______________________________ Using map symbols, Comprehension

Spanish Explorers and Conquistadors

After Christopher Columbus sailed to the Americas in 1492, Spanish soldiers called *conquistadors* (kahn KEES tuh dorhrz) and Spanish explorers crossed the Atlantic searching for gold and new trade routes. Read the map to answer the questions.

Map Key

- ·········· **Ponce de León 1513** Searched for fountain of youth. Called new land "Florida."
- • • • • • **Balboa 1513** Explored Central America
- ▬ ▬ ▬ **Cortés 1519–1521** Led conquest of Aztecs in Mexico.
- — · — **Cabeza de Vaca 1528–36** First Spaniard to explore what is now Texas.
- ——— **Pizarro 1531–33** Conquered Inca empire.
- —- - - — **De Soto 1539–1542** First European to see Mississippi River.
- — — — **Coronado 1540–1542** Explored American Southwest

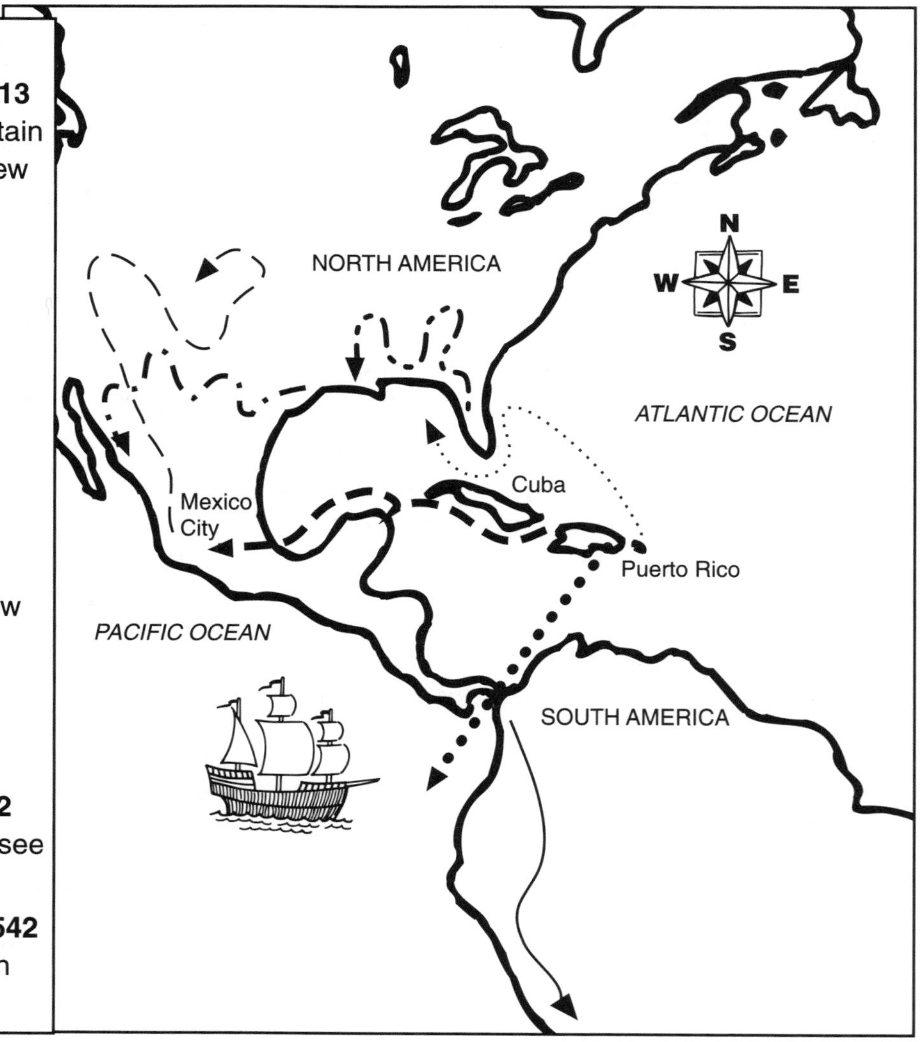

NORTH AMERICA
N
W
E
S
ATLANTIC OCEAN
Cuba
Mexico City
Puerto Rico
PACIFIC OCEAN
SOUTH AMERICA

1. From where did Ponce de León start his voyage to Florida? ______________________________

2. Where did Francisco Coronado search for gold? ______________________________

3. Which explorer's expedition ended in Mexico City? What did he do there? ______________________________

4. Write two map questions. Trade papers with a friend and answer the questions.

Name _____

Around the World

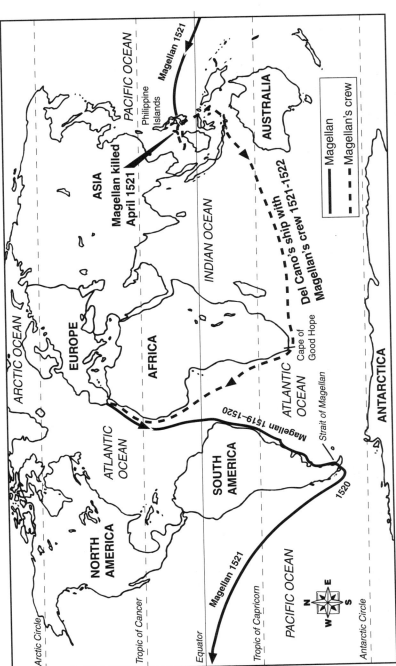

A **historical map** shows where past events took place. This map shows something that happened almost 500 years ago. In 1519, Ferdinand Magellan left Spain with five ships to find a new route to Asia. At the southern tip of South America, he sailed into a stormy, narrow waterway. It was a shortcut to the Pacific Ocean. It's now called the *Strait of Magellan*. Having found a new passage to Asia, he sailed on to the Philippines, where he was killed in a local war. Juan Sebastián del Cano sailed the crew back to Spain. Out of 241 sailors, only 18 survived the voyage. They were the first people to sail around the world!

Study the map. Read each statement. Write **T** if it's **true**. Write **F** if it's **false**. Rewrite each false statement on the back of this paper so that it's true.

_____ 1. When Magellan left Spain, he sailed to the Cape of Good Hope.

_____ 2. The new passage to Asia was at the southern tip of South America.

_____ 3. The crew crossed the equator just twice sailing around the world.

_____ 4. It took three years for the entire voyage to be completed.

_____ 5. Magellan did not get the chance to sail across the Indian Ocean.

_____ 6. Magellan sailed his ships along the coast of North America.

J332004 Clearly Social Studies

Life on a Spanish Mission

A **mission** is a settlement where Spanish priests, or missionaries, taught Native Americans the Roman Catholic religion. The Spanish built missions in the West and Southwest. They offered Native Americans food, clothing, and shelter in exchange for working on the farms and ranches and in the workshops.

Native Americans joined the missions for different reasons. Some thought the priests had religious power. Some liked the gifts the priests gave them. Others were forced to work there. Sometimes children were made to live at the missions so that their parents would join them. Soldiers carried out severe punishments, such as beatings or even death, for breaking the rules. Many Native Americans ran away.

Study this map of a Spanish mission. Answer the questions on the back of this paper. Then write four more questions about the map. Trade questions with someone.

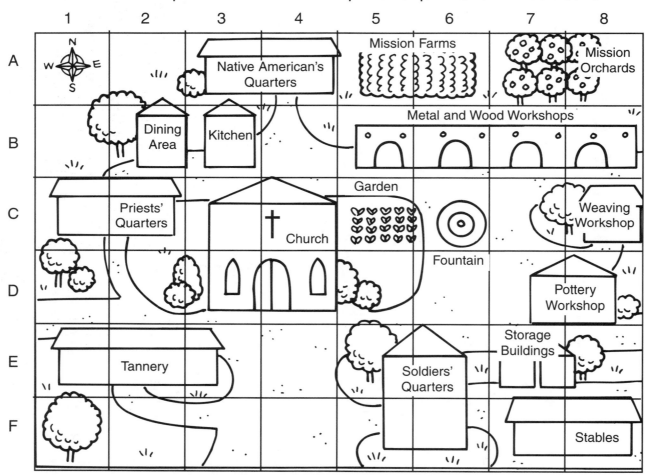

1. What is at positions C-1 and C-2?
2. What is east of the tannery?
3. At what grid position is the fountain?
4. What is west of the mission farms?
5. How many grid squares does the church cover?
6. At what grid position is the kitchen?
7. What is just north of the fountain?

J332004 Clearly Social Studies

Fighting for North America

In 1750, most of land in North America was claimed by Great Britain, France, and Spain. (Native Americans claimed ownership of land, too.) Sometimes, more than one country claimed the same land. Fighting broke out when the British tried to force the French off disputed land. The French convinced some of the Native Americans to help them fight. That is why this conflict was called the French and Indian War. France won many battles, but Britain won the war after sending its best generals, equipment, and troops to help.

Use the historical maps to answer the questions. Write on the back of this paper.

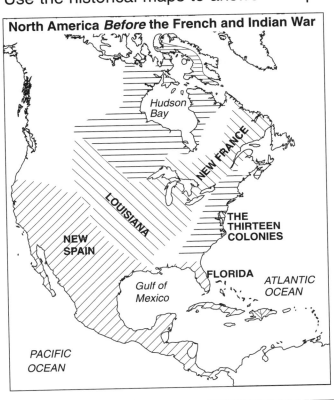

Great Britain   Spain   France   Disputed or Unclaimed land

1. Before the war, which country claimed the West and Southwest?

2. Before the war, which country claimed the colony of Florida?

3. After the war, which country claimed Florida?

4. Just before the end of the war, France gave much of the Louisiana Territory to another country in order to keep it out of British control. Which country was this?

5. Compare how much land was claimed by Great Britain before and after the war. How did the war change North America?

6. What might have happened to North America if France had won the war?

Name _____

Breaking Away From British Rule

1619	1620	1735	1773	1775
Jamestown	Cape Cod	New York City	Boston Harbor	Lexington

Jamestown
Colonial leaders of Virginia (House of Burgesses) meet to make colony's laws for printing money, building roads, collecting taxes.

Cape Cod
Before going ashore, Pilgrims write Mayflower Compact—an agreement to make and obey laws for Plymouth colony.

New York City
Printer John Peter Zenger publishes true stories about dishonest British governor; is jailed, tried, and freed; wins colonial support for freedom of speech.

Boston Harbor
Colonists fight against taxes Britain forces them to pay on British tea; they dress as Mohawks, secretly board British ship, and dump 342 chests of tea into harbor.

Lexington
Paul Revere rides to warn colonists of British soldiers who are coming to attack; American Revolutionary War begins.

Study the time line. Answer the questions in complete sentences on the back of this paper.

1. In what year did the leaders of Virginia first meet to begin steps toward making their own laws for the colonists?

2. What happened near the shore of Cape Cod a year after the House of Burgesses met?

3. How many years before the American Revolution began did the colonists fight against Britain's taxes on tea?

4. Do you think it was right for John Peter Zenger to be jailed for what he did? Why or why not?

5. Each event on the time line helped the colonists achieve their goal of governing themselves. Why do you think it was important for the colonists to make their own laws?

Name _____

The American Revolution

During the Revolutionary War, many colonists, called Patriots, wanted independence from England. Other colonists, called Loyalists, did not. Many African American slaves refused to support the war. Some of them joined with England because the British promised to free any slaves who helped them. Some fought with the Patriots because many northern colonies adopted plans to end slavery.

Read the viewpoints below. Each person is fictional, yet he or she represents a different viewpoint during the Revolutionary War. Choose one. Answer that person's questions as if you were speaking to that person. Write on the back of this paper.

"I am Mary Sanders from New Jersey. I am a proud Patriot! I don't want to be a *British* American. England makes us pay more and more taxes. The British will not let us be part of their government and help make the laws. If we work to build the colonies, shouldn't we be allowed to make our own laws? Should we be forced to give food and shelter to the British soldiers? Why do we have to pay taxes to England just to buy newspapers and tea? Our taxes should go to us! Isn't it right to want our freedom? Won't we be better off if we govern ourselves?"

"I am Thomas Jones from New York City. I am a Loyalist, a citizen of England. The king has a right to rule us. He paid for our voyages. He sends us food and supplies. He sends soldiers to protect us. Besides, the British are strong. There are too many of them to fight. My parents still live in England. Will they be harmed if I fight against England? Who would run a new government? The rich Patriots?

Bah! They'd be worse than the British! Wouldn't a government set up by the Patriots soon fall apart? Aren't we better off with England's protection?"

"I'm Sarah Marron. I'm 10 years old. I was born a slave in Virginia. My mother says that her family was taken from her home in Africa and sold into slavery. My daddy thinks that if we help the Patriots, maybe they'll help end slavery. After all, they're fighting for what we want—freedom! He says that some colonies wrote plans to end slavery. If the Patriots win, my family could run away to those colonies. We could be free! But the British soldiers tell us that if we help them, they'll free us. What should we do? Which side should we help? Will the war really end slavery? I'm so scared."

J332004 Clearly Social Studies

Declaration of Independence

After the start of the Revolutionary War, the Second Continental Congress met in Philadelphia to plan a way to protect the colonies. The delegates decided to form a new Continental Army with troops from every colony. George Washington was chosen to be commander in chief. They set up a post office, with Ben Franklin as postmaster general, so that news could be shared. They planned to make peace with Native Americans to stop them from joining the British army. They set up a committee of five men to write a document of independence for the united colonies.

Thomas Jefferson was asked to write it. He was only 33 years old. He wrote his first draft in two days. John Adams and Franklin made a few changes, and then it was brought before Congress. For three days, Congress debated over the document and made changes. Delegates softened the attacks against King George. They took out Jefferson's words about the cruelty of slavery. On July 4, 1776, the Declaration of Independence was adopted. The first delegate to sign it was John Hancock. He wrote his name big so that King George could see it without wearing glasses! The delegates knew that by signing this declaration, Great Britain would call them traitors.

The Declaration announced America's independence from England, but it took a war to finally win it in 1783. American Patriots were inspired by the Declaration, which said that all men are created equal and have the right to "life, liberty, and the pursuit of happiness."

Work with a partner. Read each statement below. Talk about whether you agree or disagree with it. On the back of this paper, write **agree** or **disagree**. Write why.

1. The Second Continental Congress didn't accomplish very much.

2. Setting up a post office in the colonies was important.

3. Thomas Jefferson was an important delegate.

4. The Continental Congress didn't want to help the colonists.

5. The delegates were brave to sign the Declaration of Independence.

6. The Declaration didn't make a difference in breaking away from Great Britain.

7. It was important to state the rights of the colonists in the Declaration.

8. July 4th is truly the birthday of the United States.

Name _____

The Constitution of the United States

After the Revolutionary War, the former colonies experienced change. Some states set up their own governments. Soon, there were different constitutions, laws, taxes, and money systems. Some states didn't accept money printed by other states! People thought of themselves as citizens of one state and not all states.

On May 25, 1787, delegates from 12 of the 13 colonies met. (Rhode Island refused to send delegates because it opposed enlarging the national government.) They voted George Washington president of their convention. They set out to plan a central government with three parts—a legislative branch to make laws, an executive branch to carry out the laws, and a judicial branch to decide what the laws meant. After months of debating, the delegates finally agreed on a set of laws. On September 17, 1787, this important document was signed by 39 men, including George Washington and Ben Franklin.

The Constitution set up how the new central government was to be run. The Constitution is still the basis of our government. The original document is displayed in an airtight, shatterproof case in Washington, D.C.

Read each statement. Write **true**, **false**, or **not stated**. If false, rewrite the statement as true. Use the back of this paper.

_____ 1. The states went through many changes.

_____ 2. The Constitution was written in Philadelphia.

_____ 3. George Washington was voted commander in chief.

_____ 4. Washington asked that the meeting be held in secret.

_____ 5. The Constitution set up a government with four branches.

_____ 6. James Madison is called the "Father of the Constitution."

_____ 7. The Constitution is the basis of our government now.

_____ 8. The original Constitution was destroyed in a fire.

Write two of your own statements. Trade with a pal. Write **true**, **false**, or **not stated**.

Rights, Rights, Rights

Read these statements that tell the story of the Constitution and its difficult road to approval. If a statement is a fact, write *fact*. If it is an opinion, write *opinion*.

_____ 1. Nine out of the 13 states needed to approve, or ratify, the Constitution before it could go into effect.

_____ 2. Citizens from small states are less important.

_____ 3. A central government might be too powerful.

_____ 4. A central government could solve the country's problems.

_____ 5. In 1787, debates over the Constitution began.

_____ 6. Leaders published their points of view.

_____ 7. People who supported the Constitution were "Federalists."

_____ 8. People against the Constitution were "Antifederalists."

_____ 9. Patrick Henry was a great speaker for the Antifederalists.

_____ 10. Antifederalists were right in wanting a basic bill of rights.

_____ 11. Almost every state had its own bill of rights.

_____ 12. In 1788, nine of the 13 states ratified the Constitution with the promise that a bill of rights would be added.

_____ 13. In 1791, a bill of rights was added as amendments.

_____ 14. There are 10 amendments that make up the Bill of Rights.

_____ 15. The Constitution is one of the most important documents in the world.

_____ 16. The United States was the first country to have the people write its constitution.

The First U.S. President

George Washington was born in 1732 on a plantation in Virginia. At age 22, he was placed in charge of a troop of soldiers and fought bravely against the French and Indians. At 26, Washington married a widow named Martha Custis, who had two children, Patsy and Jack. Washington raised the children as if they were his own.

When the Revolutionary War began, Washington was elected commander in chief of the Continental Army. He insisted that he not be paid. His army wasn't trained like the British troops. It was made up of farmers, businessmen, and hunters. After eight hard years of fighting, the British surrendered. In a tearful goodbye, Washington quietly hugged each of his officers who had served him so long.

After the war, Washington was happy to be at home in Virginia. But in 1788, when the new Constitution was ratified, the delegates elected Washington to be the first president of the United States! On April 30, 1789, he took his oath of office in New York City. This was the nation's capital at the time. He wore a plain brown suit made of cloth woven in Connecticut. From then on, Washington only wore clothes made in America. At his inauguration, Washington swore to "preserve, protect, and defend the Constitution of the United States." Presidents still say this oath today. Washington and first lady Martha then visited every state. They wanted to make all Americans feel a part of one country. Washington served two terms, refused to run for a third term, and retired to his plantation home. On December 14, 1799, Washington died at the age of 67. In his will, Washington ordered that his slaves, who he treated kindly, be freed upon his and his wife's death. Washington is often called "the Father of His Country."

Choose one question. Write your answer on the back of this paper. Support your opinion with information and facts from the story above.

1. Washington was described as "first in war, first in peace, and first in the hearts of his countrymen." Do you think this was a true description of him or not?

2. Washington was doing so well and he was so well liked by Americans. Do you think he should have served a third term and not retired after two terms?

3. What makes a good president? Do you think Washington measures up to your description? Why or why not?

A TIME OF GROWTH

Lead your students through a study of some of the famous people in American history who have provided us with such a rich heritage.

Famous American Bookmarks

Have each student make a bookmark of a famous American by following these directions:

Materials:

- 2½" x 19" strip of tagboard (one per student)
- ribbon or yarn
- hole punch
- scissors
- markers and pencils

Directions:

1. Choose a famous person— someone who has made a difference in America.
2. Use books, magazines, and other references to find one or two interesting facts about your person.
3. Write your fact in the form of a question at the top of the tagboard strip to make your bookmark. (*Did you know that Daniel Boone earned the nickname "the pathfinder"?*)
4. Illustrate the middle of the bookmark.
5. Under the illustration, write one or two sentences that describe your facts in more detail.
6. Laminate your bookmark. (*Optional*)
7. Punch a hole at the top of the bookmark to make a tassel.

Biography Booklets

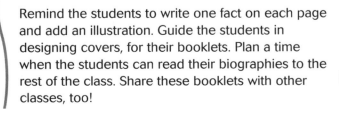

Ask the class to help you list famous Americans. See if the students can tell you why each person is famous. Then assign pairs of students different famous Americans to research. Have them then write short, illustrated biographies of the people. Write the following outline on chart paper to help the students organize their research.

I. Name of person
II. Date of birth
   A. Childhood
   B. Schooling
   C. Family memories
III. Major achievements
IV. Older years/death

After the students have gathered their information, let each pair of students make a biography booklet by following these directions:

Materials:

- 12" x 18" sheet of white construction paper
- scissors
- stapler
- pencil and markers

Directions:

1. Fold the paper into eighths. Unfold it.
2. Refold the paper in half widthwise.
3. Cut on the middle fold halfway down the paper.
4. Open the paper. It should have a slit through the middle.
5. Fold the paper in half lengthwise. Push the ends in toward the middle.
6. Push until the first and third folds meet, and fold the pages together.
7. The booklet now has eight pages. Staple the left edge.

Remind the students to write one fact on each page and add an illustration. Guide the students in designing covers, for their booklets. Plan a time when the students can read their biographies to the rest of the class. Share these booklets with other classes, too!

Will the REAL _____ Please Stand Up?

Place your students in groups of three to play this exciting game. Assign each group a famous American you are studying. Have each group research facts about its person. Tell the groups to secretly decide which one of their members will be the *real* person. (This student will give correct facts about the famous person when asked questions by the class. The other two students will give incorrect facts.) Choose a group to play first. Have each player sit in a chair behind a table. Assign each player number 1, 2, or 3. Write these numbers on separate cards and stand them up on the table in front of the appropriate players. Tell the class that it has five minutes to ask the players questions to uncover which one represents the real famous American. You play the host and call on individuals to ask the questions. At the end of the time limit, have the class vote on who they think is the real person. Then say: *Will the real famous American please stand up?* Reward the players who stump the class!

Web Mapping

Display Transparency 4, *Web Mapping*. Make a master copy of this transparency and use it to create copies of a web map for your students. Try the following activities:

- As the students study the variety of famous Americans, have them compile information about each person on their web maps. Review information by writing the name of a famous American in the center of a web on your transparency. Ask for volunteers to fill in the map.

- Have the students use the web maps to plan oral reports comparing two famous Americans.

- Play a review game. Place your students in small teams. Have teams take turns coming to the overhead. Write the name of a famous American on a web map. Give the team three minutes to fill in the web. If the team completes the web within the time limit and the information is correct, give the team five points. Take off one point for each incorrect fact. Erase the transparency and let a new team fill in the web for a different famous American. The team with the most points wins!

Student banner

Place the students in small groups. Have each group choose someone in American history who has made or is making a positive difference in our country. (For example: George Washington, Thomas Jefferson, Phillis Wheatley, Daniel Boone, Tecumseh, Meriwether Lewis, William Clark, Sally Ride) Give each group time to research its person, list his or her achievements, and design a large banner on butcher paper. Tell the students that each banner should include the name of the person honored, a portrait of the person, a list of the person's most prominent achievements, and any illustrations that depict those achievements. Have each group design a bold border for its banner and attach a length of yarn for hanging. Let each group explain its banner before you hang the banners around the classroom for a bold, informative display!

Name _____

Jefferson Expands the U.S.A.

Read about Thomas Jefferson. Complete the time line. Illustrate each event.

In 1801, when Thomas Jefferson became President, there were 16 states. France had just obtained from Spain the land between the Mississippi River and the Rocky Mountains, which it called "Louisiana." The powerful French general Napoleon Bonaparte (nuh POH lee un BOH nuh pahrt) had already taken over much of Europe. Jefferson feared that Bonaparte would also take over more land in America. In addition, the important Louisiana port city of New Orleans had been suddenly closed to American shippers. So Jefferson offered to buy the city. France answered by saying, "How much would you give for *all* of Louisiana?" What a surprise! In 1803, the United States paid France $15 million for Louisiana. This was about 4¢ an acre! It was called the Louisiana Purchase.

In 1804, Jefferson chose his assistant Meriwether Lewis to lead an expedition into Louisiana and beyond to the Pacific Ocean. Lewis asked his friend William Clark to help him. Because of this expedition, settlers had an easier time moving west. Jefferson was a President who truly helped expand the United States.

▰▰▰ 1801 ▰▰▰▰▰▰▰▰▰▰ 1803 ▰▰▰▰▰▰▰▰ 1804 ▰▰

Thomas Jefferson	_____	*Lewis and* _____
Becomes _____ *President*	*Purchase*	*Expedition*

Jefferson fears that the French general

_____

_____

will take over more land

for _____ in

America.

The United States buys this large area of land for

$_____ .

This purchase doubles the size of the United States for about

_____¢ an acre!

Jefferson funds an expedition led by his assistant

_____

to explore

_____

and the land beyond to the

_____ .

Lewis and Clark Go Exploring

A very famous event in American history is the Lewis and Clark Expedition. President Jefferson had asked his assistant Meriwether Lewis to explore the land west of the Mississippi River in search of a Northwest Passage to the Pacific Ocean. Lewis and his friend William Clark set out in three boats on May 14, 1804, with a group of about 42 men. There were soldiers, trappers, scouts, and one slave. They traveled over 8,000 miles of trails for about two and a half years.

Clark was a cartographer, a map maker. He used a large blank map to record their route and fill in the geography. Many Native Americans that Clark met shared their knowledge about the land. Some drew maps of their own for him.

When they wintered in what is now North Dakota, they met a French trapper named Charbonneau (SHARHR buh noh) and his Shoshone wife, Sacagawea (sah kah jah WEE uh). Lewis and Clark asked them to join their expedition. They wanted Sacagawea to translate for them when they traveled through Shoshone lands.

By the time they returned to St. Louis in 1806, Lewis and Clark had recorded much information about the land and its people, wildlife, plants, and geography. They had mapped more than 3,000 miles of the journey. These maps made it much easier for settlers to follow the trails out west.

Often we learn about historical events through the diaries that people write. Six of the men with Lewis and Clark kept diaries. Read the diary entries below. Notice the spelling and the language. Rewrite one of the entries as if you were writing it today. Draw an illustration for it.

> *Some of the high knobs are covred with grass. A fiew Scattering pine trees on them. the River crooked Shallow and rapid. Some deep holes where we caught a number of Trout.*
>
> —*Sergeant John Ordway describes an area near the Missouri River*

> *Great joy in camp we are in View of the Ocian, this great Pacific Octean which we been so long anxious to see. and the roreing or noise made by the waves brakeing on the rockey Shores my be heard distictly.*
>
> —*William Clark describes sighting the Pacific Ocean after the fog lifted by the Columbia River*

Going on an Expedition

Imagine that the President of the United States has sent you to explore an area in your state. You have just returned and the President has asked you to report what you have learned from your trip. Follow these directions:

- Choose an area to research. "Hike" through reference sources to study its geography, wildlife, and plants.

- To help you organize your information, answer the questions below.

- Draw a picture or map of the area.

- Write your report in paragraph form on another sheet of paper. Include facts and use your imagination, too!

- Practice giving your report orally with lots of expression. Be ready to present your report to the "President" and to your class.

1. What area in your state did you explore? _____

2. What special clothing or equipment did you need? _____
   _____

3. How did you explore the area? Did you hike, drive, use a boat? _____
   _____

4. How long were you gone? _____

5. What lakes, mountains, or other landforms did you find in the area? _____
   _____
   _____

6. What kinds of wildlife did you see? _____
   _____

7. What kinds of plant life did you find? _____
   _____

8. What interesting thing did you learn about the area? _____
   _____

9. How did you keep records of your trip? _____

10. Would you enjoy going there again? Tell why or why not. _____
    _____
    _____

The Pathfinder

Daniel Boone is perhaps the most famous of America's frontier heroes. He was born November 2, 1734, in Pennsylvania. Growing up on his family's farm, young Daniel loved to hunt and walk in the wilderness. By 12, he was a skilled rifleman. He never went to school, but he learned to read and write.

As a young man, Daniel married Rebecca Bryan, who was as good a shot as her husband! Whenever Daniel was away on hunting trips, Rebecca guarded their children and home.

Daniel explored, trapped, and hunted throughout the Appalachian Mountains. Because he was so skilled at finding trails, he earned the nickname "the Pathfinder."

Daniel and other pioneers worked to expand Native American trails from Virginia to Kentucky. The new trail they cut is called the Wilderness Road. Many pioneer families used the Wilderness Road to move west. At the end of the trail, Daniel and his men built the settlement of Boonesborough. This is where he moved his family. Daniel was once captured by Shawnees and adopted into their tribe. While living with the Shawnees, Daniel learned of their plan to attack Boonesborough. Daniel escaped in time to warn the settlers! The Shawnees couldn't capture the fort and left in peace.

Daniel served in the Virginian government and became a sheriff and a surveyor. Later, he moved his family to Missouri. He lived there until his death at the age of 86.

Use complete sentences to answer the questions.

1. What did Daniel like to do as a boy? _____

   _____

2. How did Daniel earn his nickname? _____

   _____

3. What two states were connected by the Wilderness Road? _____

   _____

4. How did the Wilderness Road help America's growth? _____

   _____

   _____

5. What do you think the Native Americans thought about the Wilderness Road?

   _____

   _____

Name _____

Two Presidents Named James

Read about two United States presidents who helped America grow stronger.

In 1809, James Madison became President. France and Great Britain were at war and wanted America's support. Madison wanted America to stay out of their quarrel. This angered both countries. They started taking American ships at sea. The British kidnapped American sailors and made them serve in their navy!

Congressmen called "War Hawks" wanted America to declare war on Great Britain. In 1812, Congress did. Known as the War of 1812, this war took place on land and at sea. In one battle, the British burned down Washington, D.C. In another, after a night of British bombardment, Francis Scott Key saw the American flag still waving! It inspired him to write "The Star-Spangled Banner." A peace treaty was finally signed, but no one won the war.

In 1817, James Monroe became President. After the War of 1812, the United States began a time of peace and growth. Yet Monroe worried that France, Great Britain, and other European countries might try to take over more land in North or South America. Because of his fears, Monroe created the Monroe Doctrine. It stated that the United States was against any takeover of land in the Americas by European countries. It also stated that the United States wouldn't participate in any future European wars.

Americans were hopeful about their future as an independent nation. They felt strong. Monroe believed that Americans formed a great family with the same interest. The United States was in a time known as the "Era of Good Feelings."

Read each phrase. Write **Madison** if it describes Madison or his presidency. Write **Monroe** if it describes Monroe or his presidency. Write **both** if it describes both.

_____ 1. the French and British were at war

_____ 2. worried about countries claiming American land

_____ 3. the War of 1812 started

_____ 4. set up a policy that America wouldn't join Europe in future wars

_____ 5. believed Americans made one great family

_____ 6. wanted America to stay out of war

_____ 7. the War Hawks were in Congress

_____ 8. helped America stay independent

Work with a partner to write your own song about our country. Use the tune from "The Star-Spangled Banner." Write it on the back of this paper. Practice singing it!

Jackson Brings Growth and Tears

Andrew Jackson grew up on the **frontier** with little education. Because he was a tough soldier, as hard as hickory wood, people nicknamed him "Old Hickory." When Jackson ran for President in 1828, it was the first time that *all* white men over 21 (and not just property owners) could vote. More people voted than ever before! Jackson won by a **landslide**. Great crowds watched his **inauguration** and cheered to see "the People's President" take his **oath** of office.

In the early 1800s, some Native American groups were **flourishing**. The first written Cherokee alphabet was **developed**

by Sequoyah. He had worked 12 years to create it. Thousands of Cherokee learned to read and write their own language. But Jackson believed that Native Americans **threatened** the settlers in the southeast. Congress passed the Indian Removal Act. It stated that the president could remove Native Americans from their land.

In 1831, the U.S. **government** began forcing Native Americans to leave their homes. Some refused. Some were taken into slavery. Jackson sent soldiers to drag Cherokee from their homes, burn their houses, and load the people onto wagons. The soldiers forced more than 15,000 Cherokee to march 800 miles away from their homeland to what was called Indian **Territory**. One out of four people died on that **march**, known as "the Trail of Tears."

Write each **boldface** word from the story beside its meaning.

1. a promise _____

2. created _____

3. doing well _____

4. was a danger to _____

5. winning an election by many votes _____

6. the act of moving at a steady pace _____

7. remote area with few people _____

8. part of U.S., yet not a state _____

9. group of people who govern a country _____

10. ceremony of placing someone in office _____

A Changing Way of Life

Help your students discover the challenges America faced as a new country—inventions that changed people's lives, pioneers who headed West, and more.

Transportation Express

Explain to the students that in America, steamboats, steam-powered trains, and other new forms of transportation helped move people and products faster, farther, and easier. Place the students in small groups. Have each group design a new form of transportation that families can use and that is also good for the environment. Tell the students that each group is to provide a detailed description of its vehicle, an illustration, and the reasons it is "Earth friendly." If possible, give each group small, empty boxes; craft sticks; buttons; and other materials to make a model of its design. Let each group present its futuristic mode of travel to the rest of the class.

Pioneer Stenciling

Tell the students that a popular way that pioneers decorated their homes and household items was by stenciling. They made their own paint by mixing skim milk with powdered colors, lime and linseed oil. On the chalkboard, draw samples of pioneer designs as shown.

Then have each student make a stenciled pencil holder by following these directions:

Materials:

- strip of tagboard to cover an empty tin can
- empty tin can
- ruler
- pencil
- glue
- scissors
- 3" x 3" square of stiff cardboard
- thick tempera paint
- paintbrush
- newspaper

Directions:

1. Copy a pioneer design or make a small one of your own on the cardboard square.
2. Cut out the inside of the design to make your stencil.
3. Trim the tagboard strip so it covers the can when it's glued completely around the can.
4. Cover your work space with newspapers.
5. Lay the tagboard strip on top of the newspapers. Position your stencil at one end of the strip.
6. Hold the stencil in place firmly and paint over your design. Paint from the outside of your stencil in.
7. After the design has been filled in, carefully lift up the stencil so that the paint doesn't smear.
8. Reposition the stencil where you want the next design to appear. Be careful not to put the stencil on top of the newly painted design.
9. Continue stenciling until you have a pattern.
10. When the paint is dry, glue the strip around the can for a handy stenciled pencil holder!

The Underground Railroad

Help your students learn more about the life of a slave by reading books such as the following:

- *Follow the Drinking Gourd* by Jeanette Winter (Knopf, 1988)

- *Which Way to Freedom?* by Joyce Hansen (Walker and Company, 1986)

Talk with your students about what it must have been like to be a slave trying to escape on the Underground Railroad. Discuss how it must have felt for slave families to hide out, walk in the night, wonder which white families along the way would help them, be chased by "slave catchers" and dogs, and finally cross the border into the North.

Place your students in small groups. Have them imagine that they are slaves escaping to the North. Tell the groups to write a story together describing one day along the Underground Railroad. Remind the students that each group member needs to contribute. Let the groups read their stories to the rest of the class.

Web Mapping

Transparency 4

Display Transparency 4, *Web Mapping*. Make a master copy of this transparency, and use it to create web maps for each of your students. Try the following activities:

- As the students study the Industrial Revolution, have each person complete one of the web maps using this central question:

    - *What helped bring about the Industrial Revolution?*

- Have pairs of students use the web maps to plan an oral report describing a 20th-century invention or new machine and the effects it has had in America.

Let individuals and partners transfer the information from their web maps onto the transparency so that the rest of the class can see it.

Zip! Pop! Inventions

Student drawing and description

The Bed Maker

Remind the students that during the 18th and 19th centuries, many different machines were invented—spinning jenny, cotton gin, electric lamp, successful steam engine, steam locomotive, riding plow. Tell the students that these inventions changed the way people lived and worked. Then place the students into groups of two. Have each pair design a new invention that will change the way many people live and work. Have each pair draw a large picture of the invention and write a detailed description of what it does and how it will change lives. Encourage the students to build models of their inventions. Let the students tell about their inventions and then post the drawings and descriptions on a bulletin board.

Name _____

The Industrial Revolution

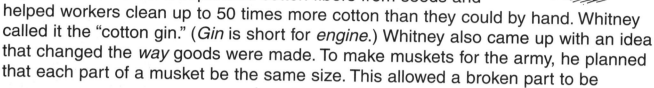

During America's early years, most people lived on farms or in small towns. Goods were made by hand in workshops or in homes. People grew their own food and made their own clothing.

Later, different kinds of machines were invented that changed the way people made goods. Eli Whitney invented one of the most important machines. It separated cotton fibers from seeds and helped workers clean up to 50 times more cotton than they could by hand. Whitney called it the "cotton gin." (*Gin* is short for *engine*.) Whitney also came up with an idea that changed the *way* goods were made. To make muskets for the army, he planned that each part of a musket be the same size. This allowed a broken part to be replaced by another part the same size. All of these interchangeable parts could be made at the same time!

Factories were built to house the new machines. People went to work in the factories to run the machinery. Production of goods increased. Costs decreased. But people worked long hours. Often men, women, and even children worked up to 14 hours a day, six days a week, for little pay.

Machines for farming were also invented. Cyrus McCormick was a Virginia farmer who built a new kind of reaper. Its sharp blades could cut and harvest up to 12 acres of wheat a day. By hand, farmers could only harvest 2 or 3 acres of wheat a day. McCormick also planned interchangeable parts for his reapers. Because of the Industrial Revolution, more people moved to the cities. They began working in factories instead of on farms. Many people enjoyed being able to buy factory-made goods.

Answer these questions in complete sentences on the back of this paper.

1. Before the Industrial Revolution, where were most goods made?

2. How did Eli Whitney's cotton gin bring a change in the way cloth was made?

3. Why were interchangeable parts so important in changing the way goods were made?

4. A revolution is a complete change. What was the Industrial Revolution?

5. Were people's lives better after the Industrial Revolution? Tell why or why not.

6. Some people say the Industrial Revolution is still going on today. What modern invention or machine do you think is changing the way people live or work?

Moving Right Along . . .

In the 1800s, many Americans and goods traveled by land. The best dirt roads were paved with logs or rocks. When it rained, roads got muddy. Travel by land was slow. People and goods also traveled by water in canoes and flat-bottomed boats. Floating log rafts had a hard time going upstream against the current. An American artist named Robert Fulton changed all this. He designed a steamboat. It had two large paddle wheels and was powered by steam. Soon, steamboats began moving people and goods quickly and cheaply from one place to another.

Travel by water became important. One of the most famous waterways was the Erie Canal. This grand canal took eight years to build. It let boats travel 350 miles from Lake Erie to the Hudson River in New York. It carried farm products to New York and goods and settlers to the West. New York City became America's biggest port and city. Soon, there was a surge of canal-building in America.

Then a new invention brought steam power to land travel. At first, railroad cars were pulled by horses on iron rails. This made travel by rail slow. With the invention of the steam-powered locomotive, trains became a quick way to carry heavy loads long distances. Train travel saved time and helped open up new lands. It provided new jobs for people. It helped connect our country.

Complete the cause-and-effect sentences. Use words from the story.

1. Travel by land was slow because _____

_____

2 Going upstream against the current made _____

_____

3. Because of the invention of the steam engine, _____

_____

4. After the Erie Canal was a success, _____

_____

5. Because of the steam-powered locomotives, _____

_____

6. When travel by trains became popular, _____

_____

Pioneers Go Far West

Early in the 1800s, fur trappers made trails out of ones used by Native Americans. Forts built on the trails gave protection and supplies to the pioneers heading west.

Write the name of each route beside its description. Follow the directions.

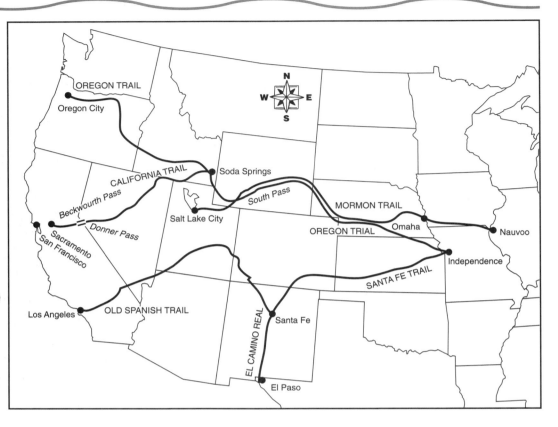

1. This is one of the longest trails. It stretched about 2,000 miles from Missouri to a fort in the Pacific Northwest. About 300,000 pioneers traveled on it. Trace it in green.

2. This trail was named for the religious group of people who traveled from Nauvoo through the Great Plains to settle near a large salt lake. Trace it in brown.

3. Pioneers on the Oregon Trail who wanted to head to California took this trail. It was hard going over the mountain passes. Trace it in yellow.

4. Some pioneers carried goods to be traded for Mexican silver and gold. They used this trail that went from Independence to Santa Fe. Trace it in purple.

5. This trail started in Mexico and led to Santa Fe. Its name means "the royal road" in Spanish. Trace it in red.

6. This trail connected Santa Fe with Los Angeles. It was basically a mule path. Trace it in orange.

The Rush for Gold!

In 1848, a carpenter named James Marshall saw something yellow shining at the bottom of a river in California where he and his men were working. "It made my heart thump," he said. "I was certain it was gold." He was right!

By 1849, thousands of people from all over the world were rushing to the West. Some lucky miners struck it rich. Most just found hard work. They spent all day in a stream panning for gold or searching for it in gravel beds. Merchants built more shops and boarding houses to accommodate all these new people. As more and more people came west, they charged higher prices for food, lodging, and supplies. Merchants got rich off the miners, who spent their money on food and supplies. The miners ended up going back home broke, without any gold. But the rush for gold made California the fastest-growing region in the nation. San Francisco, which had been a small town, became a busy city. By 1850, California had become a state!

Use the information above to answer the question and create a web map.

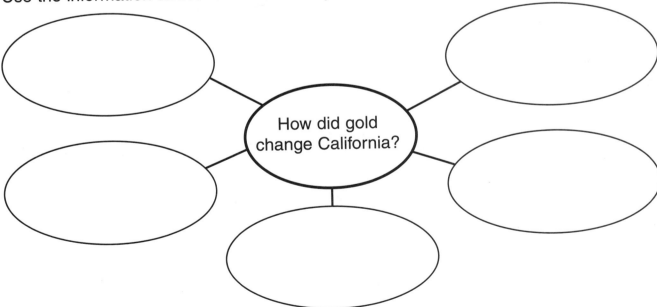

How did gold change California?

EXTRA ACTIVITY! Work with a partner. Imagine you are miners seeking gold in California. On a large sheet of paper, write to your family about your experience. Tell whether you struck it rich or are coming home broke. Illustrate your journal entry.

The War Between the States

In the 1850s, life in the South was very different from life in the North. Land in the South was good for farming. Wealthy Southerners owned large cotton plantations and used many African American slaves to do the work. About 4 million slaves worked on these plantations. Yet most Southerners owned small farms and didn't own slaves.

The colder climate in the North and the lack of fertile land made farming difficult. So instead of farming, most people worked in factories and shops. Working conditions were poor and unsafe. People worked long hours at low wages. Even though most Northern states outlawed slavery, life for free African Americans was hard. They couldn't vote or enter certain restaurants and hotels. They were pursued by "slave catchers" who searched the cities for escaped slaves.

People began to speak out against slavery. One great speaker was Frederick Douglass. He was a slave who had secretly learned to read and write and had escaped to the North. Women began to speak out against slavery, too. Harriet Tubman, an escaped slave herself, led slaves along secret routes to freedom in the North. These routes were called "the Underground Railroad."

In 1861, some Southern states formed a new country called the Confederate States of America, or the Confederacy. They had their own flag and elected their own president—Jefferson Davis. President Abraham Lincoln believed the states didn't have the right to secede, or break away, from the Union. He felt strongly that all the states should stay united. The North and the South went to war! After four years, the South finally surrendered. Both sides suffered heavy losses. About one out of every 50 Americans died in the war. The debate over slavery had ended, and the North and the South were once again united.

Read each phrase. Write **N** if it describes the North. Write **S** if it describes the South.

_____ 1. President Jefferson Davis _____ 6. good farm land

_____ 2. factories and shops _____ 7. unsafe working conditions

_____ 3. large plantations _____ 8. seceded from the Union

_____ 4. had "slave catchers" _____ 9. had 4 million slaves

_____ 5. the Confederacy _____10. won the war

At the time of the Civil War, most people in the North and the South didn't believe that African Americans were equal to them. Yet many people in the North were against slavery. Why do you think this was so? Write on the back of this paper.

Rebuilding a Country

The South needed to rebuild after the Civil War. Much of it was destroyed and its people harbored bad feelings. Many freed slaves had no work or homes. And, a few days after the war, John Wilkes Booth shot and killed President Abraham Lincoln! This time in history is called the Reconstruction.

When Vice President Andrew Johnson became president, he began to rebuild the South. He helped to pass the 13th Amendment to the Constitution, which abolished slavery.

Congress also had a plan to rebuild the country. It provided food, clothing, shelter, and other needs to both blacks and whites who were homeless and without work. It set up schools. It passed the 14th Amendment, which said blacks were United States citizens with the same rights as whites. It passed the 15th Amendment, which said people couldn't be stopped from voting just because of their skin color or race.

Many freed blacks and poor whites became sharecroppers. They rented and worked the land owned by others. Often these workers borrowed money to buy supplies and paid the landowners by giving up as much as half their crops.

When Reconstruction ended, the new Southern states passed laws to separate blacks and whites. Both races couldn't use the same hotels, restaurants, trains, schools, or even drinking fountains! Many Southerners turned to violence to frighten African Americans away from their homes. The war gave African Americans citizenship, but they still didn't have equal rights.

Write the word from above that best completes each sentence.

_____ 1. Reconstruction meant to _____ the South.

_____ 2. The 13th Amendment _____ slavery.

_____ 3. The 14th Amendment said blacks were U.S. _____ .

_____ 4. The 15th Amendment gave blacks _____ rights.

_____ 5. _____ rent land for a share of the crops they grow.

_____ 6. Some southerners turned to _____ to scare freed slaves.

Work with a partner. Talk about why you think the South had a difficult time accepting freed slaves as equals. Choose to be from the North or the South. Together write a letter to an imaginary newspaper called the "Reconstruction Times." Try to convince readers that freed slaves should have equal rights. Read your letter to the class.

STUDYING ANY STATE

By studying your home state in connection with other states and the world, your students will become more aware of what's special about where they live.

Start With What We Know

Begin a study of your state by displaying a large outline of it on butcher paper. (Use Transparency 5 on page 61 for a pattern.) Ask the students what they know about their state—its capital city, national parks, rivers, major cities, etc. Pinpoint these on the map and write their names. List any facts the students know around the outline. Display the map during your study, adding new facts as you go along.

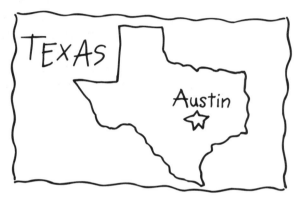

State Connection

Transparencies 5, 7, 8

Have your students compare your state with other states and with the world. Share books such as the following:

- *American Grub: Eats for Kids From All Fifty States* by Lynn Kuntz and Jan Fleming (Scholastic, 1997)

- *Facts About the 50 States* by Sue R. Brandt (Franklin Watts, rev. ed. 1988)

- *Fabulous Facts About the 50 States* by Wilma S. Ross (Scholastic, rev. ed. 1986)

Display Transparency 5, *The United States*. Have a student draw a star on the map to identify your state. Ask the students: *Which region is your state part of? Which states border it?* Then place Transparency 7, *Latitude and Longitude,* on top of the United States map. Review the use of these lines by having a student trace specific lines of latitude and longitude with a finger. Show the students how the lines on this map are in increments of 10. Model how to use these lines to locate places. Let students practice using lines of latitude and longitude to

identify states. Ask questions such as *In which state do the lines of 40°N latitude and 110°W longitude intersect?* (Utah) Next, display Transparency 8, *World Physical Map*. Help your students locate North America. Let different students describe the geographic area of your state and its surrounding states. Help the students find other geographic areas around the world that compare to your state.

New Plates for Your State

Have your students design new license plates for your state. Remind the students what your state's current plates look like. Have your students help you list on chart paper what's special about your state that could be illustrated on a license plate. Then give each student a large rectangular sheet of white paper. Have the students design new license plates that graphically illustrate the unique features of your state.

State Sing-a-longs

Place your students in small groups and have them write verses to a song about your state. Have each group begin and end its verse using the following:

"Our State's Great"
(Sung to the tune of "Three Blind Mice")

Our state's great,
It's first rate!
Our state's great,
Make no debate.

(For the verse, use words and phrases that describe landforms, places, cities, and other things that make your state special. Example:
Rocky Mountains and rivers galore,
Mines of copper and iron ore,
History filled with frontier lore, . . .)

Oh, our state's great,
It's first rate!

Fill-in-the-State Fun

Transparencies 5 & 6

Reproduce Transparency 5, *The United States*. Make a class set of blank maps. Give each student a blank map. Display Transparency 5 on the overhead. Place the students in two groups. Challenge each group to correctly identify as many states as possible within a given time limit (10 to 20 minutes). Have the students use pencils to write in the state names on the maps as the states are identified. When the time is up, call on individuals from each group to take turns identifying a state on the transparency map and saying its name. Write the state's name on the transparency. Have the students check their answers. Keep a tally of how many states each group correctly identified. (Reward the winning group by letting it go out to recess first!)

Use Transparency 6, *United States Political Map,* as an overlay to Transparency 5. Have the students write in the rest of the names of the states that they weren't able to identify. Tell the students to use this completed map as a reference guide during your study of the United States.

Twenty Questions

Transparency 6

Display Transparency 6, *United States Political Map*. Help the students learn the state capitals by playing Twenty Questions. Have a student think of a capital city. Let the remaining students ask up to 20 questions that can be answered with *yes* or *no*. The student who guesses correctly thinks of the next one.

Myself as a State

Have the students design maps of themselves as new states! Tell the students to draw large outlines of themselves on butcher paper. Have each student list hobbies; family members; likes; dislikes; and favorite colors, food, etc. Tell the students to base their state names on their own names. Have them use their personal information to label capital cities, major cities, rivers, lakes, towns, airports, and other major landforms on their maps. Encourage the students to be creative in designing their maps. Display these unique maps for all to admire!

Photograph of Reporters Presenting Their "Great State News"

Note cards

Place the students in small groups to write and perform "TV" news reports about why their home state is a great place to live. Brainstorm with your class topics to choose from for the state reports—history, capital city, recreation, wildlife, major landforms, products, etc. Have each group choose a different topic to create a five-minute TV news report. Have the students research their topics so they can write accurate information on their "teleprompters" (note cards). Encourage the students to watch TV news broadcasts for inspiration. Give the groups ample time to plan and rehearse their news shows. Remind them to draw visual displays (maps, illustrations, etc.). If you can, videotape each show so the students can watch their performances and take turns sharing the video with their families. Photograph each group. Display these photos on a bulletin board. Display each group's note cards and visuals (if possible) next to its photo.

State Reference Chart

STATE	CAPITAL	NICKNAME	ABBREVIATION	JOINED UNION
Alabama	Montgomery	Heart of Dixie	AL	1819
Alaska	Juneau	Last Frontier	AK	1959
Arizona	Phoenix	Grand Canyon State	AZ	1912
Arkansas	Little Rock	Land of Opportunity	AR	1836
California	Sacramento	Golden State	CA	1850
Colorado	Denver	Centennial State	CO	1876
Connecticut	Hartford	Constitution State	CT	1788
Delaware	Dover	First State	DE	1787
Florida	Tallahassee	Sunshine State	FL	1845
Georgia	Atlanta	Empire State of the South	GA	1788
Hawaii	Honolulu	Aloha State	HI	1959
Idaho	Boise	Gem State	ID	1890
Illinois	Springfield	Land of Lincoln	IL	1818
Indiana	Indianapolis	Hoosier State	IN	1816
Iowa	Des Moines	Hawkeye State	IA	1846
Kansas	Topeka	Sunflower State	KS	1861
Kentucky	Frankfort	Bluegrass State	KY	1792
Louisiana	Baton Rouge	Pelican State	LA	1812
Maine	Augusta	Pine Tree State	ME	1820
Maryland	Annapolis	Old Line State	MD	1788
Massachusetts	Boston	Bay State	MA	1788
Michigan	Lansing	Wolverine State	MI	1837
Minnesota	St. Paul	Gopher State	MN	1858
Mississippi	Jackson	Magnolia State	MS	1817
Missouri	Jefferson City	Show Me State	MO	1821
Montana	Helena	Treasure State	MT	1889
Nebraska	Lincoln	Cornhusker State	NE	1867
Nevada	Carson City	Silver State	NV	1864
New Hampshire	Concord	Granite State	NH	1788
New Jersey	Trenton	Garden State	NJ	1787
New Mexico	Santa Fe	Land of Enchantment	NM	1912
New York	Albany	Empire State	NY	1788
North Carolina	Raleigh	Tar Heel State	NC	1789
North Dakota	Bismarck	Flickertail State	ND	1889
Ohio	Columbus	Buckeye State	OH	1803
Oklahoma	Oklahoma City	Sooner State	OK	1907
Oregon	Salem	Beaver State	OR	1859
Pennsylvania	Harrisburg	Keystone State	PA	1787
Rhode Island	Providence	Ocean State	RI	1790
South Carolina	Columbia	Palmetto State	SC	1788
South Dakota	Pierre	Mount Rushmore State	SD	1889
Tennessee	Nashville	Volunteer State	TN	1796
Texas	Austin	Lone Star State	TX	1845
Utah	Salt Lake City	Beehive State	UT	1896
Vermont	Montpelier	Green Mountain State	VT	1791
Virginia	Richmond	Old Dominion	VA	1788
Washington	Olympia	Evergreen State	WA	1889
West Virginia	Charleston	Mountain State	WV	1863
Wisconsin	Madison	Badger State	WI	1848
Wyoming	Cheyenne	Equality State	WY	1890

Teacher: Play "State Scavenger Hunt." Place the students in pairs. Challenge them to be the first team to find the answers to questions about the chart. (e.g., *Find the two state nicknames with the word <u>green</u> in them!*)

Name _____

United States Map

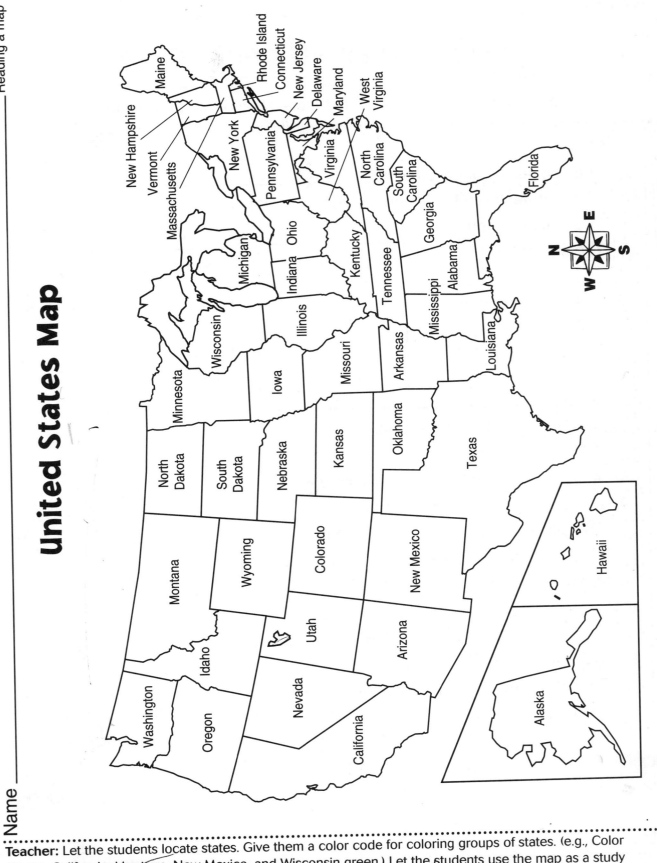

Teacher: Let the students locate states. Give them a color code for coloring groups of states. (e.g., Color Alaska, California, Montana, New Mexico, and Wisconsin green.) Let the students use the map as a study guide. Then have them try to fill in as many state names as they can on copies of Transparency 5 (page 61).

47
reproducible

Name ______________________________ Research, Recording information

State Poster Planning Guide

Use books and encyclopedias to fill in the facts. Make a poster about your state.

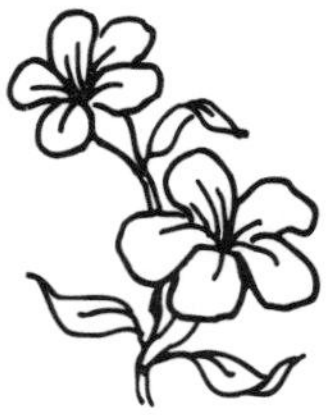

1. My state's name is ______________________________.
2. The capital city of my state is ______________________.
3. This state entered the Union (became a state) on ____________.
4. The state nickname is ______________________________.
5. The state bird is ____________________.
6. The state flower is ____________________.

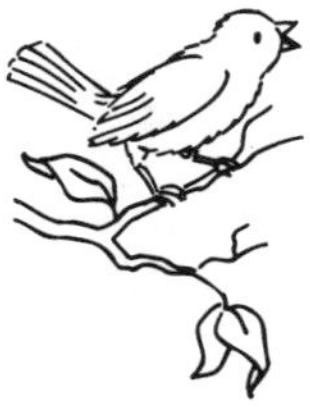

State Bird

State Flower

7. A tourist attraction in this state is ______________________________ ______________________________.
8. A natural resource found in this state is ____________________.
9. A product grown in this state is ____________________.
10. The city with the largest population is ____________________.
11. The area (size in square miles) of this state is ______________.
12. A river, lake, or forest found in this state is ______________ ______________________________.
13. An animal that lives in this state is ____________________.
14. The state tree is ______________________________.
15. Something interesting about this state is ____________________ ____________________ ____________________ ____________________.

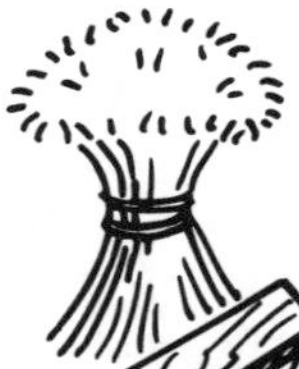

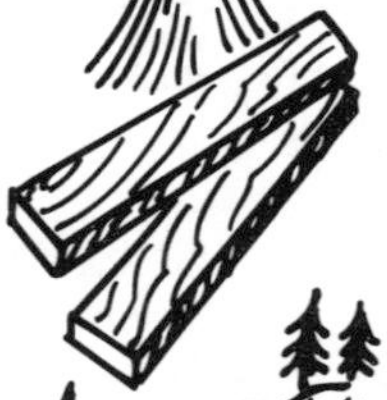

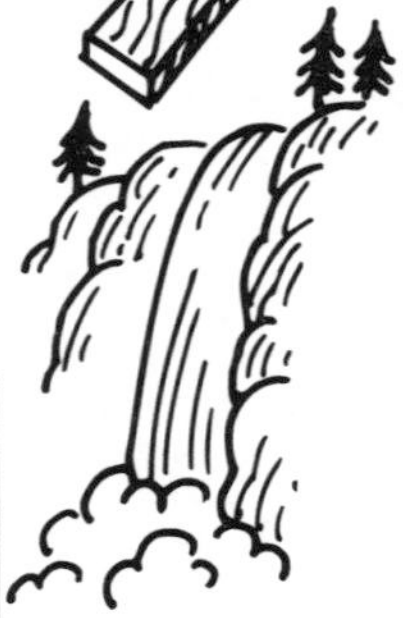

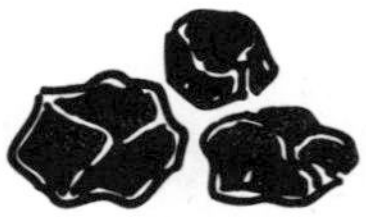

Animal

State Tree

Teacher: Assign small groups or individuals different states or your home state. Give them time to research and write the needed information on this plan. Let them take turns sharing their state posters.

State Map Grid

Many maps have a grid—lines that form a pattern of boxes. A grid helps you locate places quickly on a map. On the grid below, draw your home state. Include the capital city and major rivers, mountains, valleys, deserts, lakes, and cities. Then on the back of this paper, write five questions about your map grid. (For example: *Which city is in box B4? Which mountain is in box D5?*) Switch papers with a classmate and answer each other's questions. Check the answers together.

	1	2	3	4	5	
A						A
B						B
C						C
D						D
E						E
	1	2	3	4	5	

Name ______________________________ Comprehension, Research

State Flag

Each of the 50 states has its own flag. On it are colors and symbols that represent something special about that state. Imagine that Greenwall is a state and below is its state flag. Follow the directions to complete the flag.

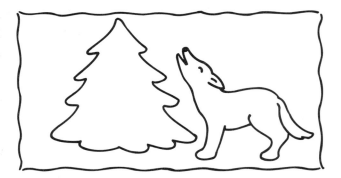

The tree stands for Greenwall's large Pinewood Forest. Color the tree **green**.

Greenwall is known as the Wolf State. Color the wolf **brown**.

Color the background of the flag **blue**. The blue stands for the many lakes in Greenwall.

Find out about your state's flag. Then answer these questions.

1. What colors are on your state flag? ______________________________

____

2. What symbols or pictures are on it? ______________________________

____

Draw your state flag in the box. Color it.

Write the name of your state.

____

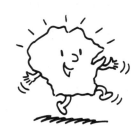

If you think your state flag represents your state really well, write why.

____

____

____

If you think your state should have a new flag, design one. Draw it on the back of this paper. Write what the colors and pictures mean.

Teacher: A great resource for state flags is *How Proudly They Wave* by Rita Haban (Lerner, 1989).

A Road Map

A road map shows you how to get from one place to another. It shows cities and highways. Sometimes it shows points of interest and the number of miles between places. Use the map of Colorado to answer the questions in complete sentences.

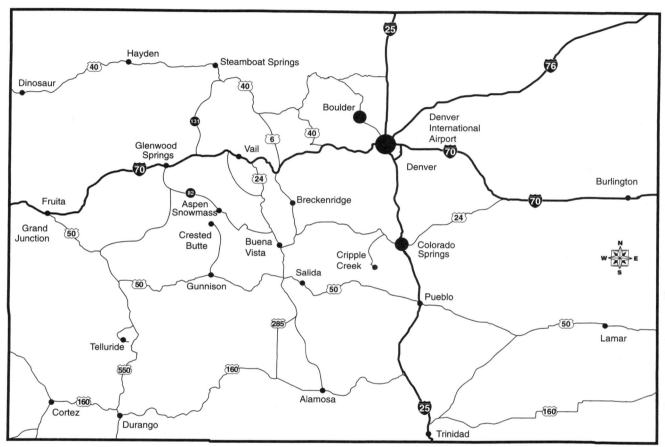

1. Which highways provide the most direct route between Grand Junction and Aspen? _____

2. Using different-colored pencils, trace the shortest and longest possible routes between Steamboat Springs and Breckenridge. Which highways did you not trace? _____

3. If you drove northeast from Colorado Springs on highway 24 to interstate 70 and then drove west on 70, to which city would you be driving? _____

   _____

4. What are two ways you might travel to get from Grand Junction to Pueblo? Give highways and direction of travel. Write both ways on the back of this paper.

5. Write your own question about the map. Have a friend answer it.

Name ____________________ Group work

State Group Work

Work in a group of four students. Decide who will be *Reader* (reads the questions), *Recorder* (writes the group's answers), *Artist* (draws the group's pictures), and *Monitor* (makes sure each group member contributes; turns in the project).

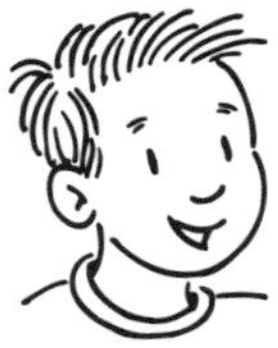

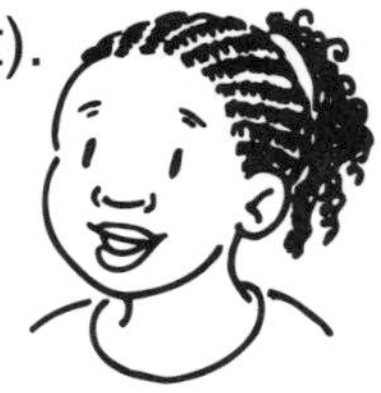

Group Members

Reader ____________ Recorder ____________

Artist ____________ Monitor ____________

Answer any two questions. Be ready to share your answers with the class.

1. What do people in your state do for fun? Talk about your answers. Write two of your best answers.
2. What makes your state so special? Is it the geographic features? the history? the goods it produces? Talk over your thoughts. Write the answer the group likes best.
3. Which groups of Native Americans live or have lived in your state? Write one of the group's names. Write something about this group.
4. How is your state changing? Are more highways being built? Are more parks being constructed? Will the changes make the state a better place to live or a worse place to live? Talk about your answers. Write a group response.

Group Record Sheet

( ) ____________________

( ) ____________________

Choose one project to do as a group. Be ready to share your project with the class.

- ☐ Write a group letter to the governor of your state telling him or her about how to make your state a better place to live.
- ☐ Write and perform a song or poem about why your state is great.
- ☐ Draw a large picture showing an important event in your state's history. Write a few sentences below your picture describing the event.

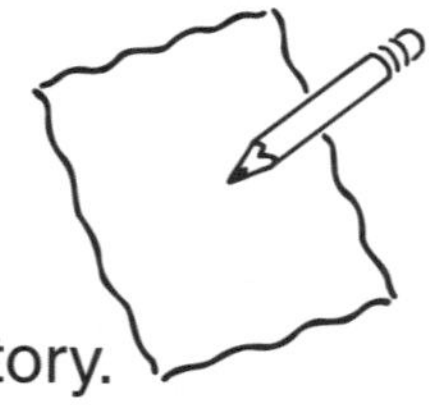

Create a State

Imagine that you are a cartographer (someone who makes maps). You are given the assignment to make a map of a new state! Answer the questions below to help plan your map. Draw a rough draft of your map on the back of this paper. Include a scale of miles, a compass rose, and a map key. Make a larger final version of your map neatly on another sheet of paper. Label your map. Color its features.

1. What kind of thing is your state shaped like? Choose one. Describe its shape.

   ☐ animal   ☐ plant   ☐ landform (lake, mountain)   ☐ object

   _____

2. Where is the state located (near which ocean or other state)?

   _____

3. What is the name of the state and its capital city?

   _____

4. What are the major landforms in the state (rivers, mountains, lakes, bays, etc.)?

   _____

   _____

5. What are some special parks, airports, and other points of interest that you will include on your map? _____

   _____

6. What is the state flower, state bird, state motto, and state tree? _____

   _____

   _____

7. Write about the feature—such as wildlife, recreation areas, climate, or cities—you like best about your state.

   _____

   _____

   _____

   _____

   _____

ANSWERS

Page 6

7. The Southwest region has the fewest states.

8-10. Answers vary.

Page 7

Natural Resources of the United States Regions				
REGION	FOSSIL FUELS	FORESTS/PLANTS	MINERALS	WILDLIFE/FISH
WEST	Oil	Birch Cedar	Lead Zinc	Deer Salmon
MIDWEST	Oil Coal	Maple Sunflowers	Copper Iron	Deer Bass
SOUTHWEST	Natural gas Oil	Cacti Oak	Iron Copper	Rabbit Shrimp
NORTHEAST	Coal	Maple Spruce	Copper Granite	Quail Lobster
SOUTHEAST	Natural gas Coal	Pine Mangrove	Iron Salt	Ducks Shrimp

Page 8

Natural Resources	Usefulness/ Value	Things That Threaten	How to Protect/ Conserve
Fossil Fuels	heat our homes run our vehicles and machines	people are using them up fast	set limits, conserve
Forests	soak up sunlight, produce oxygen, made into paper goods	insects and diseases, acid rain	limit the chemical we use, recycling
Soil	crops, plants, and trees are grown in it	planting too many crops, acid rain	use less chemicals, control the amount of crops

Page 9

1. The name of this line is the Continental Divide.
2. Salt Lake City, Utah, is near a large lake.
3. Mt. McKinley is the name of the tallest U.S. mountain.
4. The Missouri River flows near the capital of Montana.
5. Death Valley and the Mojave Desert are two deserts in the Great Basin.

Page 10

1. You would travel about 400 miles.
2. Austin, Texas, is about 200 miles from where the Rio Grande and Pecos rivers meet.
3. You would end up visiting the Painted Desert.
4. You wouldn't have reached Austin, Texas.
5. You could explore the Colorado River (or the Grand Canyon).
6. You would travel about 800 miles to get from Phoenix to Oklahoma City.

Page 11

1. It would be the same time (10:00 a.m.) in Des Moines, Iowa.
2. It would be 4:00 p.m. in Indianapolis, Indiana.
3. It would be 6:00 a.m.
4. North Dakota, South Dakota, Kansas, Michigan, Indiana, and Nebraska all have two time zones.
5. I would phone her at 8:00 p.m.

Page 12

1. New Orleans
2. Mississippi River
3. 80°W and 90°W
4. Lake Okeechobee
5. Jackson
6. Question varies.

Page 13

1. south
2. west
3. Trenton
4. Vermont, Massachusetts, Connecticut
5. Dover
6. Washington, D.C.
7. Question varies.

Page 16

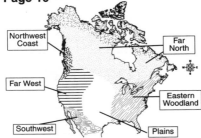

Page 18

1. Ponce de León started his voyage to Florida from Puerto Rico.
2. Francisco Coronado searched for gold in the American southwest (North America).
3. Cortés's expedition ended in Mexico City, where he conquered the Aztecs.

Page 19

1. F
2. T
3. F
4. T
5. T
6. F

Wording may vary for each false statement that has been rewritten:

1. When Magellan left Spain, he sailed to South America.
3. The crew crossed the equator four times sailing around the world.
6. Magellan sailed his ships along the coast of South America.

Page 20

1. The Priests' Quarters are at C-1 and C-2.
2. The Soldiers' Quarters are east of the tannery. So are the storage buildings and stables.
3. The fountain is at C6.
4. The Native Americans' Quarters are west of the mission farms.
5. The church covers four grid squares.
6. The kitchen is at B3.
7. The Metal and Wood Workshops are just north of the fountain.

Page 21

1. Spain claimed the West and Southwest.
2. Spain claimed the colony of Florida.
3. Great Britain claimed Florida.
4. France gave Spain much of the Louisiana Territory.
5. Wording varies. Possible answer: By winning the war, Great Britain claimed most of North America from Canada to Florida.
6. Answer varies. Possible answer: If France had won the war, it would have claimed the British colonies and Canada. We might be speaking French instead of English! We might not have become the United States, an independent country.

Page 22

Wording varies for each answer.

1. In 1619, the leaders of Virginia first met to make laws for the colony.
2. In 1620, the Pilgrims wrote the Mayflower Compact.
3. Two years before the American Revolution began, the colonists fought against Britain's tea taxes.
4. Answer will vary.
5. Answer will vary.

Answers

Page 24

Wording varies for each statement of support.

1. disagree—The delegates formed a new Continental Army, made George Washington commander in chief, set up a post office with Ben Franklin as postmaster general, planned how to make peace with Native Americans, and set up a committee to write a document of independence for the colonies.
2. agree—By setting up a post office, the colonists could share news about events going on around them.
3. agree—Thomas Jefferson was an important delegate because he wrote the Declaration of Independence!
4. disagree—The Continental Congress did want to help the colonists. It wanted to plan ways to protect them with a new Continental Army and to set up a way to share news by establishing a post office.
5. agree—The delegates were brave to sign the Declaration of Independence because by doing so Great Britain would see them as traitors and would probably threaten their lives.
6. disagree—The Declaration probably made the most difference in breaking away from Great Britain. It stated that the colonies were free, it united the colonists, and it established a citizen's rights.
7. agree—By stating the colonists' rights, the Declaration united the colonists as one nation. Listing the rights helped everyone know what their rights were as an independent nation.
8. agree—July 4th is the birthday of the United States, because it was on this date that the Declaration of Independence was adopted. It was the first official announcement of independence from Britain.

Page 25

1. true
2. not stated
3. false
4. not stated
5. false
6. not stated
7. true
8. false

Wording may vary for each false statement that has been rewritten:

3. George Washington was voted president of the convention.
5. The Constitution set up a government with three branches.
8. The original Constitution is displayed in an airtight, shatterproof case in Washington, D.C.

Page 26

1. FACT
2. OPINION
3. OPINION
4. OPINION
5. FACT
6. FACT
7. FACT
8. FACT
9. OPINION
10. OPINION
11. FACT
12. FACT
13. FACT
14. FACT
15. OPINION
16. FACT

Page 30

1. 1801—Thomas Jefferson Becomes **Third** President: Jefferson fears that the French general **Napoleon Bonaparte** will take over more land for **France** in America.
2. 1803—**Louisiana** Purchase: The United States buys this large area of land for $**15 million**. This purchase doubles the size of the United States for about **4¢** an acre!
3. 1804—Lewis and **Clark** Expedition: Jefferson funds an expedition led by his assistant **Meriwether Lewis** to explore **Louisiana** and the land beyond to the **Pacific Ocean**.

Page 31

Answers vary. Possible answers:

Some of the high knobs (hills) are covered with grass. There are a few pine trees scattered on them. The crooked river is shallow and the water is moving rapidly. There are some deep holes where we caught a number of trout.

There is great joy in camp! We can view the Pacific Ocean. We have been anxious for so long to see this great Pacific Ocean. The roaring and noise made by the waves breaking on the rocky shores may be distinctly heard.

Page 33

1. Daniel liked to hunt and walk in the wilderness as a boy.
2. Daniel earned his nickname because he was so skilled at finding trails.
3. The Wilderness Road connected Virginia and Kentucky.
4. Answer varies. Possible answer: The Wilderness Road helped America's growth by creating a way for pioneers to settle in the West.
5. Answer varies. Possible answers: The Native Americans might have thought that the pioneers didn't have a right to take over their trails.

Page 34

1. Madison
2. Monroe
3. Madison
4. Monroe
5. Monroe
6. both
7. Madison
8. both

Page 35

1. oath
2. developed
3. flourishing
4. threatened
5. landslide
6. march
7. frontier
8. territory
9. government
10. inauguration

Answers

1. oath
2. developed
3. flourishing
4. threatened
5. landslide
6. march
7. frontier
8. territory
9. government
10. inauguration

Page 38
1. Before the Industrial Revolution, most goods were made in workshops or in homes.
2. Answer varies. Possible answer: Eli Whitney's cotton gin made it possible for workers to separate cotton much faster than by hand.
3. Wording varies. Possible answer: Interchangeable parts were important in changing the way goods were made because they could all be made at the same time. A broken part could immediately be replaced with a same-sized part.
4. Wording varies. Possible answer: The Industrial Revolution was a change in the way people made goods and where they worked— from goods made by hand to machine-made goods; from working on farms to working in factories.
5. Answer varies.
6. Answer varies.

Page 39
Answers vary. Possible answers:
1. Travel by land was slow because **the roads were dirt and often paved with only logs or rocks.**
2. Going upstream against the current made **moving goods on log rafts difficult.**
3. Because of the invention of the steam engine, **travel by boat became quick and cheap.**
4. After the Erie Canal was a success, **New York City became America's biggest port and city.**
5. Because of steam-powered locomotives, **trains could carry heavy loads long distances.**
6. When train travel became popular, **new lands and jobs opened up.**

Page 40
1. Oregon Trail
2. Mormon Trail
3. California Trail
4. Santa Fe Trail
5. El Camino Real
6. Old Spanish Trail

Page 41

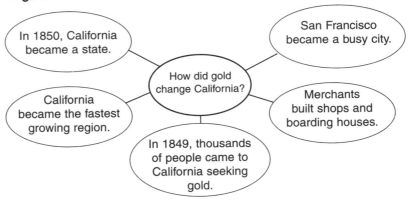

Page 42
1. S
2. N
3. S
4. N
5. S
6. S
7. N
8. S
9. S
10. N
Answer varies to question.

Page 43
1. rebuild
2. abolished
3. citizens
4. voting
5. Sharecroppers
6. violence
Answer varies for student-written letter.

Page 51
Possible answers:
1. Interstate 70 and highway 82 are the most direct route between Grand Junction and Aspen.
2. Answer varies.
3. I would be driving to Denver.
4. I could drive east on the 70 and south on the 25, or I could drive south and then east on the 50. (Many other routes are possible.)
5. Questions will vary.